W9-ART-599

鱪 をこぜ	鰈 かれい	鮹 たこ	鮨 し す
魳 いさぎ	鯵 あじ	鰹 かつを	鮪 まぐろ
鯎 うぐゐ	鮗 このしろ	鯖 さば	鯛 たい
鮲 こち	鮥 せいご	鯒 こち	鱚 きす
鮒 ふな	鯉 こい	剣 はぜ	鮭 さけ
鮖 いるか	鯑 かずのこ	鱶 ふか	鱒 ます

THE BOOK OF SUSHI

THE BOOK OF
SUSHI

Kinjirō Ōmae

Yuzuru Tachibana

Foreword by Jean-Pierre Rampal

KODANSHA INTERNATIONAL
Tokyo • New York • London

Foreword

Because of my concert career, I travel a great deal and have the opportunity to observe and experience a great variety of cultures all over the world. And I love to eat.

When I arrive in a foreign country and am taken to dinner, frequently my host invites me to a French restaurant so I will feel at home. Of course I am quite fond of French cooking, but I do not like to be chauvinistic about it. I try to establish very quickly that I'm a real traveler, that I enjoy discovering things new to me and always prefer to eat and drink the native food of the country I'm visiting. Each country's traditions and dishes offer something special to me. I like to explore. After all, I can always get fine French food at home, but I cannot always eat fried chicken as they make it in the American South, or drink *caipirinha* from Brazil or feast on *shabu-shabu* or *unagi* prepared in the Japanese way.

I have been very lucky, not only to have seen so many of the world's natural wonders, but also to be able to indulge in the culinary wonders of many different lands. One major exception, however, to my native-cuisine rule occurs when I have the opportunity to experience a sushi meal at one of the many marvelous Japanese restaurants on either coast of the United States.

I have no memory for dates, but the first time I visited Japan must have been over fifteen years ago. I fell in love with Japan at once. Both the country and her food stimulate my imagination. To me it is the most colorful nation, probably because Japan seems to have more living traditions than the other countries I've visited. Out of my milieu there, I feel like I am in a dream. Sometimes it's just like being in a fairy tale, and this I find refreshing.

At the time of my first visit, my record manager was a man from Holland who had lived in Japan for five or six years. He took me very early one morning to the Tokyo fish market at Tsukiji. Shafts of morning sunlight brightly illuminated the open-sided, high-roofed warehouses. Boxes piled high with shellfish—clams, oysters, spikey wreath shells—vied for space with bins of silvery mackerel, plump sardines and palm-sized white-sided sole. In a neat row at one end were large, whole tuna, shipped by sea or air from oceans the world over. The wholesaler was auctioning them off at a staccato rate. Some of these 6- to 8-foot beauties had already been carted by middlemen to stalls not far away, where they were being cleaned and carved, revealing the succulent red, tender flesh.

Every aisle was punctuated with

baskets of shrimp—and what a variety! Small curled shrimp looked like a cache of hoarded coins, and the large ones, I learned, practically the size of a fist, are called *kuruma-ebi*, or "wheel shrimp."

With water splashing everywhere, the aisles were like rivers, and this, together with the clean briny smell in the cool morning air, made me think of these marine cornucopias as still being alive in their natural habitat. Among the many people scurrying about in black rubber boots were vendors eager to dispose of their goods as early as possible. At the same time they kept an eye out for their regular buyers, who come daily from Tokyo's restaurants and sushi shops to obtain the freshest fish to please their discriminating clientele. All this made me eager to sample the native cuisine based on these wonderfully fresh riches of the sea.

My friend and manager introduced me to sushi. I don't recall exactly when and where, but probably in a small place in the Tsukiji district, which is famous for restaurants serving fish. I thought sushi was fabulous, absolutely fabulous, from my very first bite. The completely natural taste of fresh fish and the delicately vinegared rice on which it is served make a perfect marriage. The size is just right too—a perfect mouthful.

This was not the first time I had eaten raw fish. In Marseille on the Mediterranean, where I grew up, we regularly eat raw sea urchin. Now I have a house in Corsica and have become an avid *uni* fisherman. When I

am there on vacation, we fish almost every day and frequently pry as many as 100 of these spiny delicacies from the rocks where they live. The sea urchin near Corsica is usually a little smaller than the Japanese variety, and we prepare them differently. We cut away a piece of the shell and rinse it in fresh salt water and eat all the insides, sometimes with a piece of bread, as an appetizer before going home to dinner. Perhaps because of this, one of my favorite sushi is *uni*, although as I later discovered, in sushi only the creamy golden roe is eaten.

I think it is important not to go only to the fanciest or most expensive restaurants when in a foreign country. I myself love to eat in rather common places. There is a marvelous area near the Ginza in Tokyo, which is very colorful and popular. Here a myriad of small shops selling grilled foods like *yakitori* (skewered grilled chicken) and *okonomiyaki* (savory pancakes) has grown up among the steel and concrete supporting the elevated railway tracks. Sitting with other customers out in the open on stools and watching the crowds thread their way through this maze of steel and smoke, I was somehow transported to the past century. I sometimes get the same impression from the sight and smells of the *oden*-stew vendors who appear on the street at dusk, wheeling wooden carts, their mobile kitchens. The places I go to for sushi are often similar— small and unassuming, absolutely authentic and accessible to one and all, although I have been to very exclusive and private dining rooms too.

"Fingers" of sushi make a perfect lunch, simply because fish is fresher earlier in the day, but I often go out to eat and relax after a concert, and then I sometimes find myself going down twisting bylanes with others in the group. Eventually, ducking under an indigo-dyed quarter-length curtain and sliding open the small door, we are welcomed by a battery of chefs into a bright and sparkling clean sushi establishment.

Whether for lunch, supper or after-concert meal, in Japan I always try to sit at the counter. This means I can choose exactly the seafoods I particularly like from the delectable array. Here I can see the consummate skill that goes into the making of each order, and I can try to establish rapport with the sushi chef.

The sushi chef is truly an artist. He takes pride not only in taste, but also in his cutting skill and the visual appearance of what he serves. I have my favorite sushi combinations, of course, but I love to ask the master to come up with his own, personal creations. Usually the master falls in with my request with smiling enthusiasm. As a consequence I've enjoyed some interesting combinations in sushi shops around the world: smoked salmon and exotic roes in New York, avocado and crab in Los Angeles, and tiny whitebait in Japan. That these are individual, once-in-a-lifetime creations, I seriously doubt, but by asking the chef to innovate with the materials he has before him, I know I have an excellent taste experience, one that isn't "on the menu."

I love all sushi and I am particularly fond of *ōtoro*, the fattiest cut of tuna; *maguro*, the deep red meat of the tuna; and *anago*, sea eel boiled and served with a special sauce. It seems that I can never get enough. When I have a morsel that is particularly delicious, I often ask the chef to follow it up with one more of the same. I have my own idiosyncracies about sushi. I realize that the vinegared ginger, or *gari*, is to cleanse the palate between servings, but I prefer to do without it. And I am not overly fond of the sweetened, folded omelet which many people eat at the end of the meal as a sort of dessert. When prudence dictates that a meal is near its end, I usually close with an uncut roll of *tekka-maki*—a Japanese "ice cream cone," as some of my American friends call it.

In Japan or out, sushi is sometimes an acquired taste. I have visited Japan with my father and with my son. Both of them immediately loved sushi, so their introduction to this food was easy. My wife Françoise, however, at first did not like raw fish.

The second time I was in Japan with Françoise marked her raw fish "baptism." Wanting to show her Kyoto, I scheduled a couple of free days with no concerts. Today I can almost get by traveling with my limited Japanese vocabulary, but at that time I needed an escort. My record manager at Nippon Columbia graciously offered to help, but when he called me, he said that there would be an international convention of eye surgeons meeting in Kyoto during the time we planned to be there and that all the hotels were booked solid. He suggested, instead, staying in a Japanese home. As it turned out, this was an elegant old residence in the traditional style in downtown Kyoto, near a big temple, and was the home of a retired geisha and her even older housekeeper. They had rooms for us, and it was arranged that we would be served a dinner and breakfast.

Françoise and I were excited about being in a Japanese home, and everything went perfectly until our first breakfast. The housekeeper appeared with a traditional and beautifully arranged breakfast— including both raw fish and raw eggs! Luckily Françoise was not quite awake. When she asked what was for breakfast, cajolingly I told her it was cut fruit. She ate the fish and smiled to be polite, though I'm not sure I fooled her. Today, however, she is used to both sushi and *sashimi* (sliced raw fish).

With Françoise I also learned a good lesson about the Japanese language and its inflections. I took her to a Japanese restaurant, and wanting to impress her with all the vocabulary I knew, I confidently said, "*ka-ki*," giving the last syllable a rising inflection. The waiter bowed and left the table only to return with a persimmon. This did impress my wife, but not in the way I had intended. She knew I wanted to order oysters! I was sure I had the right word, so I repeated myself—"*kaki*"—and the polite waiter, without any change of facial expression, brought us another red persimmon. My exasperation was not helped by my wife's amused laughter. Finally, in desperation I

again asked for "*kaki*." This time, my disappointment and embarrassment influenced my inflection on the last syllable, making it droop down sadly. Voilà—Oysters!

And so I learned that even though words might be spelled the same way in romanized Japanese, they are not necessarily pronounced the same way. Oysters are not usually a sushi ingredient; they are too soft and runny. But my experience with *kaki* has made me keep my sense of humor when ordering sushi *a la carte* at the counter. I try to exercise my Japanese vocabulary, and though I'm not always sure I'll get what I think I ordered, I know I'll enjoy the experience.

The key to sushi is freshness, but how fresh is fresh?

In Nagoya I have been to a restaurant which has a tank with live fish. You can choose your own lobster. The chefs take it from the tank, remove the insides and clean it. Then they reconstruct the prepared lobster. They do the same with crayfish. Like the sea urchin whose spines still move even after there is nothing left inside it, some parts of the lobster or crayfish still move while you're eating them.

And in Sapporo on the island of Hokkaido, I've been served fish alive. The fish is like a small tuna with firm flesh. After cutting a thin fillet off the fish, the chef puts it back in the tank. It was a little difficult for me to eat while the fish was staring back at me from the tank. It didn't die. Perhaps this would be too disconcerting to a sensitive person. But thinking about it,

I came to feel that for a person who really loves fresh fish, the assurance of such absolute freshness strikes a sensible note and adds a certain pleasure to dining.

The popularity of sushi and *sashimi* is spreading. An old friend and former student of mine from Japan married a Swiss fellow, and it is he who has learned to prepare sashimi. When they visit us in Corsica, he goes to the market early in the morning. He carefully explains to the fishmonger that he is going to prepare the fish raw, then selects fresh tuna, sea bass, *daurade* (sea bream) and snappers. Home again he makes a beautiful platter of sashimi decorated with fresh flowers. It is wonderful to realize that sushi and sashimi can be prepared anywhere where fresh fish are available.

My own preference is for sushi. The wedded taste of rice and fresh fish is more satisfying to me. Increasingly, one can find restaurants featuring sushi cropping up not only in major cities outside Japan, like Paris, New York and Los Angeles, but even in smaller towns. For example, I have eaten in a marvelous Japanese restaurant, where the sushi is prepared with great skill, in Red Bank, New Jersey.

But no matter where I find a true sushi master, at that moment my heart is transported to Japan, and I know I am going to indulge in a truly perfect meal—sushi, a ritual symphony of visual and savory textures.

JEAN-PIERRE RAMPAL

1. The Sushi Shop

Edomae-zushi

As we approach the sushi shop, it is a good time to think briefly about this representative Japanese food, for isn't it true that the better we understand the things we eat and the ways they are prepared, the more we appreciate them?

A charming legend has it that long ago an old man and his wife charitably left some rice in the nest of an osprey living near their house. Later they found fish in the nest. They took the fish home, ate it and were delighted by the intriguing flavor their leftover rice had imparted to the fish as it underwent natural fermentation. This may be only a story, but it agrees with the historical account of how in ancient times vinegared rice was used to preserve fish. The fish was later eaten, the rice discarded. As time passed and the Japanese developed their cuisine and enriched it with importations from abroad, they began to eat both fish and rice, and something approaching modern sushi was created.

There are many ways to prepare sushi and it can be made at home. Three widely known types are *oshi-zushi* (pressed sushi), *chirashi-zushi* (scattered sushi) and *maki-zushi* (rolled sushi). The first is made by pressing rice and other ingredients in a mold. In the Osaka-Kyoto area where it originated and is still very popular, it features more cooked than raw seafoods. In making *chirashi-zushi*, pieces of cooked or uncooked seafood and vegetables are arranged on loosely packed sushi rice. This kind is served in bowls. In the Osaka version the ingredients are cooked, then chopped or sliced. *Maki-zushi* is made by rolling rice and other ingredients (seafoods or vegetables) in thin sheets of *nori* seaweed.

We will devote most of our attention to the sovereign of the sushi world—*nigiri-zushi*, or *Edomae-zushi* as it is called because it was first made and was once found only in Edo, as Tokyo was known before 1868. Today it is eaten all over Japan and in many other countries as well. It is made of vinegared rice and raw, marinated or cooked fish, shellfish or other toppings.

In the following pages, we present the fundamentals of sushi making, from the difficult task of selecting the right fish to the final step of forming attractive and appetizing food, after first having a look at the sushi shop itself.

Inside the Sushi Shop

"*Iras–shai, iras-shai, irasshai!*"

The voices that convey this vigorous and clear greeting the minute you walk into the sushi shop are those of the man who makes the sushi—the *itamae-san*—and his assistants. Such a greeting is not unusual in Japan, but there is something special about the one heard in the sushi shop.

The decor of sushi shops may vary from place to place and time to time, but certain items are essential to all. Most conspicuous is the spotlessly clean *hinoki* cypress counter, at the back of which, in refrigerated glass cases, are arrayed the colorful, carefully prepared fish, shellfish, vegetables and other ingredients that tempt both eye and palate. Behind the counter, ready to form bite-size servings by hand, stands the sushi chef in his starched white coat and white hat. His busy helpers may be there, too, unless they are in the kitchen, where take place the painstaking preparations which make possible the apparently effortless virtuosity of the chef's performance. The assistants have climbed the long ladder from kitchen worker to their present status and hope to become sushi chefs themselves—some day. Their training is long (at least five years) and not everyone who starts at the bottom rung makes it to the top of the ladder.

For the first-time customer, the world of the sushi shop can be a bit perplexing. He may wonder whether to sit at the counter or at one of the tables. Waiters and chefs, who are adept at judging their customers, will encourage the obvious gourmet to make himself comfortable at the counter, where he can select and enjoy his favorite sushi. Other customers may be discreetly directed to a table, where they will probably order one of the combination sets and eat and drink little else.

Unlike in ordinary restaurants, the customer in a shop serving only sushi is not offered a detailed menu after he is seated, although to simplify the task of selection, some sushi shops in Japan do post large, colored diagrams illustrating standard kinds of sushi offered almost everywhere. In the United States, solicitous shop proprietors place plastic-covered charts with pictures showing sushi types and ingredients on their tables and counters.

The reason prices are not displayed in the better sushi shops is that maintaining the highest standards depends on buying the finest and freshest fish daily. The availability of the choicest fish varies, and prices both in the fish market and the sushi shop can fluctuate from day to day.

Knowing what to order requires the experience and knowledge sushi chefs devote years to acquiring. Since the new customer can scarcely be expected to command such knowledge, the wisest entry into this world is to ask the man behind the counter what is good and rely on his judgment.

From the light shades, which resemble Japanese umbrellas, to the spotless counter to the wall beneath the counter, the sushi shop master spares no expense to make his shop attractive and comfortable.

Sake, in the red sake warmer, is drunk with appetizers before (never while or after) eating rice. The chef is placing *sashimi* on cucumber leaf. The white radish by the leaf is made by peeling off long, wide sheets of *daikon* with a knife, then slicing it into slender strips.

Dining at the sushi shop is an ideal time to enjoy good conversation, either with the shop master or one's companions. For their foreign customers, Japanese sushi shops now display signs (like the one in the background) showing various fish or types of nigiri-zushi.

How to Eat Sushi

After nigiri-zushi was created, some thought was given to convenient and appetizing ways of eating it. The preferred ways, using either the fingers or chopsticks, are described below.

Fingers

To eat sushi with the fingers:

1. Pick up the piece of nigiri-zushi with the thumb, index and middle fingers and turn it over.
2. Dip the end of the topping (not the rice) in soy sauce.
3. Place the sushi in the mouth so that the topping encounters the tongue first.

Fondness for soy sauce leads some people to soak the rice part of sushi in this seasoning. This is not recommended, since, not only will the rice fall apart, but the flavors of both topping and rice will be obliterated. Soy sauce should complement, not conceal, the foods it is eaten with.

Sushi is accompanied by thin slices of vinegar-pickled ginger (*gari*). Many people take small bites of *gari* to freshen the mouth between servings of sushi. Sushi aficionados, however, may leave out the ginger entirely, and they may even omit the soy sauce. Or they may find the following way satisfying, though it is not easy at first and takes practice:

1. Bite off half a piece of ginger and place the other half on the piece of sushi.
2. Holding the ginger in place with the index finger, take the sushi between thumb and middle finger.
3. Dip the end of the topping in soy sauce.
4. Place the whole piece of sushi in the mouth so that the topping touches the tongue first.

Pick up sushi.

Dip topping in soy sauce.

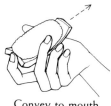

Convey to mouth.

Chopsticks

In the past sushi was considered a snack, rather than a full meal. Alcoholic beverages and other foods were never served with it. This began to change after World War II, when a few sushi shops serving *tempura* and other foods, as well as various beverages—sake, beer, whiskey and even brandy—were seen. Another change was in the place setting put before each customer when he sits down. At one time sushi counters were supplied with running water for washing the hands, but this amenity has vanished. Instead there is a small steaming towel to wipe the hands with, a simple act that also helps the diner to relax and enjoy his meal. Another towel is kept at hand throughout the meal to clean bits of food from the fingers.

There will also be a pair of wooden chopsticks in a slim white paper wrapping. Originating from a stick broken in half and used as pincers, chopsticks, which range from 21 to 36 cm. in length, are generally made of bamboo, willow, cryptomeria, Hokkaido chestnut, or cypress. Some are thick, some slender, some round, some squarish. Some taper at one end, some at both. The finest chopsticks are made from cedar grown in Yoshino, an area near the ancient capital of Nara. There, too, is a shrine dedicated to chopsticks, where a festival is held each year on April 22.

It is said that if the Japanese stopped eating with chopsticks, the wood thus saved could be diverted to building 50 thousand houses annually. Be that as it may, it is estimated that some 8 billion sets of disposable chopsticks are used in Japan each year.

The sushi shop proprietor chooses his chopsticks with his customers in mind, and his selection may be a hint to the quality of the food served in the shop.

Sashimi (sliced raw fish) or other light foods eaten as a prelude to a meal of sushi are eaten with chopsticks. Sushi itself may also be eaten with chopsticks.

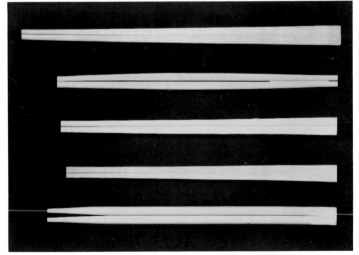

Disposable wooden or bamboo (at bottom) chopsticks come in several shapes and sizes.

The chopsticks may be joined at the top. Carefully split them apart (as shown in the illustration), then:

1. Place one chopstick in the hollow between the thumb and index finger and support it on the ring finger.

2. Hold the other chopstick with the tips of the thumb, index and middle fingers and manipulate its tip against the tip of the other one, which is held stationary.

To eat sushi with chopsticks:

1. Turn the finger of sushi on its side, gently, so that the rice doesn't fall apart.

2. Dip the end of the topping in soy sauce.

3. Convey the sushi to the mouth with the side still down.

4. As when eating with the fingers, avoid an excess of soy sauce.

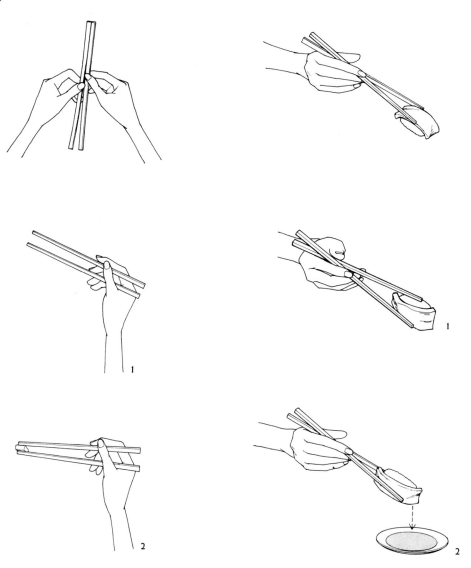

Order of Eating

There is no set order in which the various kinds of nigiri-zushi must be eaten. In Japan, a lot of people prefer to start off with *maguro* and follow it with whatever strikes their fancy. Less experienced, and even experienced, diners ask the chef what is particularly good that day. Following the chef's suggestions is a sensible way of enjoying the choicest of the day's selections.

When all sushi shops prepared *gyoku* themselves, gourmets always ordered this thick sweet omelet first, so as to have an indication of the cook's prowess. Now most shops rely on outside suppliers of *gyoku*, and its flavor may vary little from shop to shop. But each sushi shop does have its own way of preparing and serving *kohada* (gizzard shad) and *anago* eels. Ordering one of these is one way of evaluating the overall quality of a particular shop.

When a combination sushi plate is served, the *nori*-wrapped pieces should be eaten first, since the crispness of *nori* seaweed does not last long once it comes into contact with damp rice.

What to Drink

In the days when sushi shops were outfitted with stand-up counters, no sake was sold in them, since standing up was not a position conducive to relaxed imbibing.

In the modern sushi shop with its comfortable counter and tempting seafoods displayed in refrigerated cases, the diner may linger awhile over warmers of sake while nibbling *sashimi* (sliced raw fish) or other light foods. Or instead of sake, the customer may prefer beer, whiskey or even wine. Ultimately, the choice of beverage is a matter of taste, but the consensus among sushi chefs is that sake is best. Sake drinkers seem to be on the increase in the United States, where one producer alone, Ozeki San Benito, annually produces 550 kiloliters of sake in Hollister, California.

Tea

Whatever the preprandial drink, there is always green tea.

The cup of this refreshing drink served to the customer at the start of the meal is refilled as often as necessary until the meal is over. This is not merely for the sake of courtesy. Green tea is essential to the full enjoyment of sushi; sipping it removes aftertastes and leaves the mouth fresh for the next serving.

The *yunomi* cup with thick walls found in sushi shops has a long history. When sushi was sold in outdoor stalls and water supplies were limited, proprietors of these modest establishments decided it was more efficient to pour a copious draft of tea in a large, heat-retaining cup at the outset, thus reducing the number of times the cup had to be refilled.

Many sushi shops make use of powdered green tea, rather than the more common leaf tea, because it yields the characteristic color, flavor and aroma more quickly and is more convenient when large quantities are needed. Nutritionally, the vitamins

(A, B$_1$, B$_2$, C and PP) in tea nicely complement the nutrients in seafoods and rice.

Sushi Shop Vocabulary

The sushi shop can be an interesting language experience. Even the person who understands Japanese may be baffled when he first hears the words spoken by the sushi chef and his helpers, for they have their own jargon. The words heard when they are counting, for example, may even be unique to a particular shop. The following is a short selection of traditional terms.

For counting:

pin: one	*ronoji*: six
ichinoji: two	*seinan*: seven
geta: three	*bando*: eight
dari: four	*kiwa*: nine
menoji: five	*yorozu*: ten

Other terms:

agari: tea. Usually, *ocha*. (O)*agari*, signifying that a person has finished eating, comes from the language of the pleasure quarters of long ago. Originally *agari* meant only the cup of tea served at the end of the meal (the first cup was called *odebana*) but eventually came to mean tea whenever served.

gari: vinegar-pickled ginger root.

hikari-mono: things that shine. Small fish served with the scales removed but with the skin attached. E.g., *aji* (horse mackerel).

ichinin-mae: a serving for one person. The term is used to order the thick omelet eaten at the end of a meal of sushi.

ikijime: fish kept alive until shortly before time to serve.

katami-zuke: a term used when one half of a fish fillet becomes the topping for nigiri-zushi. E.g., *kohada* (gizzard shad).

murasaki: soy sauce. Usually, *shōyu*.

nami no hana: salt. Usually, *oshio*. *Nami no hana* means "flowers of the waves," a reference to the age when Japan relied on seawater as a source of salt.

nigemono: fish that are cheaper.

nojime: fish not kept alive after they are caught.

odori-ebi: "dancing shrimp." Shrimp served live.

otemoto: chopsticks. Usually, (o)*hashi*.

shari: vinegared sushi rice. Cooked rice is usually *gohan*. Buddhists treasure tiny bits of bone traditionally said to be relics of Shakyamuni, the historical Buddha. Rice grains bear some resemblance to these pieces of bone, called Buddha *shari* from a Sanskrit word.

sugata-zuke: used when a very small whole fish becomes the topping for nigiri-zushi. E.g., *tai* (sea bream).

New Menu Daily

The sushi shop is unusual in that the customer sitting at the counter can see the seafoods or vegetables from which individual servings will be made and can watch the chef deftly perform his artistic work—and enjoy a lively conversation with him at the same time. And sushi shops also differ from other restaurants when it comes to menus.

Typically there aren't any.

If the customer is inclined to worry about what the bill will come to, he can order the combination set. This consists of 7 to 9 pieces—nigiri-zushi and maki-zushi—selected by the proprietor in such a way as to allow him to offer it at a fairly stable price. It is cheaper because, like ready-made clothes, the combination set is not necessarily made piece by piece to fill individual orders. It will not be of inferior quality. The combination set is prepared by the chef and his assistants in the same way that everything in the shop is prepared.

If when he finishes the diner wishes more, he is always free to order sushi of his choice. Or a second combination set. Japanese customers usually eat no more than 10 pieces of sushi. Western appetites seem to be bigger, sometimes two or three times that of the Japanese.

There is no truth in the rumor that sitting at the counter results in a lower bill. People at the counter most often order *a la carte*, which may be likened to having suits tailor-made from the finest fabrics. The customer who orders only the freshest and the best will find that it can run into money. But this is worth remembering: sushi worth eating is never inexpensive.

Armed with a little background information, anyone, even the cautious, can enjoy the delights of sushi, and a particular restaurant will probably end up being a favorite. Without knowing it, perhaps, he may also leave a strong impression on one or more chefs. To them the know-it-all who makes unreasonable demands is a pest. They are much more partial to the guest who dines enthusiastically and keeps up his end of the frequently spirited conversation.

Adding up the Bill

One tradition of the sushi shop is the remarkable way chefs keep track of the orders filled for each customer. (No charge for the tea, of course.) They do not do it by surreptitiously lining up grains of rice, as the rumor has it. They do the reckoning in their heads, keeping accounts for as many as 5 or 6 customers at one time.

Nor is it true that chefs arrive at the total bill by estimate or charge what they think the traffic will bear. Many customers are regulars and would spot such a practice right away. Chefs calculate, with legendary efficiency, on the basis of each piece of sushi having a price of the day. Since there are 2 pieces to a serving, *all* they have to do is remember the food and drinks each customer requested, multiply, and add up the total.

Practical jokers have been known to act as if everything a group ordered was to go on one check, then ask for individual tabs at the end of the meal. The sushi chef, especially if he is a man of experience, will take it all in stride and come up with the correct figure for each member of the group.

For those who consider price no object, a sushi shop's ambience is the most important factor in deciding whether to go to one place or another. Interior decoration can play a role in this, but without doubt atmosphere depends most on the skill and personality of the man who runs the shop.

This, of course, presumes that the first requirement has been fulfilled, namely that the quality is good. No one wants to eat in a place where the food is poor, and while it is tempting to say the cheaper the better, such a viewpoint is meaningless if low prices are gained by the sacrifice of quality. As already noted, freshness is paramount, and whether with regard to seafood or other ingredients, a shop selling top-quality food once can be relied on to sell top-quality food regularly.

To sum up, it can be said of the ideal sushi shop that it is one serving food of the best selection and preparation in an atmosphere conducive to enjoyment and good digestion at prices appropriate to one's pocketbook.

2. Topping and Core

Seafoods and Vegetables

Nigiri-zushi is an extremely popular food in Japan, among young and old, rich and poor alike. The secret of its popularity is not hard to find: it allows one to savor a wide range of eye-catching delicacies, particularly from the sea but also from the land. Anything from *wasabi* horseradish from the mountains to abalone (*awabi*) from the bottom of the sea may be used in some way, so long as the ingredients harmonize with the vinegared rice on which they are served. All the ingredients are prepared in ways that allow their natural flavors, be they the most elusively delicate or the richest, to emerge at their best.

The simple foundation without which Edomae-zushi could not exist is sushi rice, or *shari*. (Its preparation is explained on p. 59.) The topping ingredients—called *tane* in Japanese—were originally fairly modest. In the early years after the creation of nigiri-zushi, the principal toppings included thick or thin omelet, abalone, small sea bream (*tai*), gizzard shad (*kohada*), whitebait (*shirauo*), the common Japanese conger eel (*anago*) and, from about 1830, tuna (*maguro*).

With changing tastes and times many varieties have disappeared from the list but many others have been added. *Shirauo*, for example, is rarely seen in sushi shops now, and the once-popular *hamaguri* clam, which was served boiled, has recently lost favor to uncooked seafoods. The fat part of *maguro*, called *toro*, was unpopular before World War II, but as the Japanese became more accustomed to eating meat, *toro* came to take pride of place over the lean red flesh. So-called *hikari-mono* (literally, "things that shine")—that is, fish served with their silvery skin intact but without scales—formerly were always marinated and were not used as sushi topping. Some of these fish are *aji* (horse mackerel), *sayori* (halfbeak) and *kisu* (sillago). Today *hikari-mono* find favor with many people.

The problem of which seafoods to eat raw, which to marinate and which to cook has been solved by the wisdom born of experience, and it is not too much to say that the Japanese have understood these matters for centuries. Fish like salmon and herring, for example, are not eaten raw, because of the possible presence of parasites, and, for the same reason, no freshwater fish are ever eaten raw in sushi. It is as safe to eat sushi as it is to eat raw clams or raw oysters.

Ingenuity has contributed to widening the range of sushi ingredients. One example is the development of the *gunkan-maki*, or "battleship wrap," for such difficult-to-contain treats as fresh salmon roe (*ikura*) and raw sea urchin (*uni*) roe. (See p. 66.)

Until modern times the sushi chef's choice of ingredients was limited by the tendency of raw fish to spoil quickly. To beat the summer heat before the days of refrigeration, they kept their seafood supplies in dark, cool holes dug under the shop floor. Modern methods of preservation and transportation now enable sushi shops to serve abalone, the round clam called *aoyagi*, and scallops raw, as well as to offer customers all over the country such once strictly regional delights as salmon and a delicate small shrimp named *sakura ebi*.

Nowadays Japanese may eat tuna airfreighted from the northeastern United States or shrimp delivered from Mexican waters. Ingredients other than seafoods have become increasingly popular, too. *Nattō*, a kind of fermented soybean, *shisō*, a plant of the mint family, *ume-boshi* (pickled plum) and avocado are recent innovations, used either as topping or as a filling for *maki-zushi* (rolled sushi). These are popular with strict vegetarians.

Maguro, Tuna

Honmaguro, tuna

Tuna, a member of the mackerel family and the most familiar of sushi toppings, comes in many varieties: *honmaguro* or *kuromaguro* (tuna), *mebachi* (bigeye tuna), *kiwada* (yellowtail tuna), *binnaga* (albacore) and so on. Needless to say, only fresh fish is prized; the canned tuna of the kind familiar in the United States is not at all suitable for sushi.

Honmaguro tuna is found in the waters off most of the shores of the main Japanese island of Honshu and as far away as the Philippines. Tuna caught off the shores of Miyagi Prefecture, called *Sanriku maguro* after that section of the Pacific Coast, is considered particularly good.

To prepare *maguro*, first the head and tail are removed. Then the flesh is cut from the spine to make two large boneless fillets. These two fillets are cut lengthwise into back (upper) and belly (lower) blocks, which are roughly triangular in cross section. Each of these blocks is called a *chō*. A shop will usually purchase one or two *chō* each day. The section of the belly block closest to the body cavity is the fatty *ōtoro*. It is expensive. Flesh somewhat less fatty than this (*chūtoro*) comes from the belly block near the tail and the back block. The flesh around the spine is lean and red; this is called *akami*. The red flesh near the tail is the least expensive.

26

In Japan tuna is best in the winter, while in the United States the tuna of summer is the most delicious. Some people find it even better than Japanese *maguro*, and the price is said to have shot up exorbitantly in connection with the recent increase in the number of sushi devotees in the United States.

A slice of *maguro* used as a nigiri-zushi topping usually weighs about 1 2 grams. In the photo below, the upper row of sushi fingers is *akami*, the lower *chūtoro*. At the right are *wasabi* root and sliced ginger.

Makajiki, Swordfish

Makajiki, swordfish

In Japan, several varieties of swordfish are used for food: *makajiki* (swordfish), *mekajiki* (broadbill), *kurokawa* and *shirokawa* (for which there are no common English names) and so on. All have the rapierlike projection of one jaw that accounts for the generic English appelation.

Highly regarded for its delicate flavor, *makajiki* was until the middle of the 19th century considered to make the very best sushi. This swordfish reaches a length of 2 meters (about 6 1/2 feet) and is found from Hokkaido to the South Pacific. The broadbill *mekajiki* grows in shallower tropical and temperate waters throughout the world.

The pink flesh of the *makajiki* is best in autumn. The creamy-colored flesh of the *mekajiki* is most flavorful in summer.

Sushi is like an almanac skillfully
gathering in knowledge of the
tastes of the four seasons.

Katsuo, Bonito

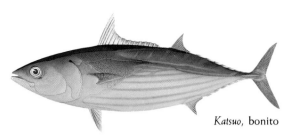

Katsuo, bonito

Like tuna a member of the mackerel family, the bonito figures in a famous verse in which the first taste of *katsuo* in season is compared with the foliage of spring and the call of the mountain cuckoo. During the Edo period (1603–1868) *katsuo* was so highly thought of that when it came into season—May in the Tokyo region—the temptation was strong to leave one's wife at the pawnbrokers and buy *katsuo* with the borrowed money. Or so the story goes.

Bonito comes largely from the waters around the southern coast of the island of Shikoku. In sushi shops, it is filleted and the flesh nearest the skin lightly grilled to make what is called *Tosa-mi*, an excellent sushi topping which is especially good when eaten with grated fresh ginger. Tosa is the name of the region in southern Shikoku where *katsuo* fishing orginated.

Tai, Sea Bream

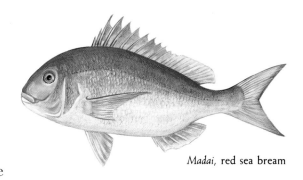

Madai, red sea bream

Sea bream was considered the pinnacle of gourmet excellence in the past, as the saying, "Even rotten, it is still *tai*," suggests. And this reputation has caused the name *tai* (or its variation *dai*) to be added to hundreds of species of fish that are not bream at all: *aodai*, *hamadai*, *medai* and many others. Besides these three, other "non-*tai tai*" appearing in nigiri-zushi include *ishidai* (parrot fish) and *himedai*.

True bream from the Seto Inland Sea is regarded as the finest in Japan, because its flesh is white and delicately flavored. Skinned fresh *madai* (red sea bream) is sliced and used as a topping for nigiri-zushi. Another way to serve it is to leave the skin on and pour hot water on the skin side to blanch it before the sushi is prepared. Still another way is to take a small whole bream, clean and bone it, and stuff the body cavity with sushi rice.

Kohada, Gizzard Shad

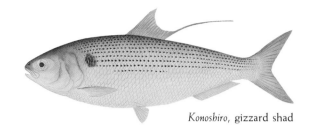

Konoshiro, gizzard shad

Kohada (gizzard shad) live near the bottom of the sea in waters off central and southern Japan. As with various species, its name changes with the age of the fish. When it is medium size and in its prime for use in sushi, it is called *shinko* or *nakazumi* (shown in the photo below). As it grows bigger, it loses the simple flavor that makes it good for sushi. It is then called *konoshiro* and may be eaten if cooked in the right way.

Marination in vinegar is essential to soften *kohada*'s many small bones before using it as a sushi topping. The bones also make it unsuitable for boiling, and it smells unpleasant when grilled.

Learning how to marinate gizzard shad is the beginning of the sushi chef's training in vinegared foods. Succeeding in this task is indicative that he has completed that phase of his training. Among the many things he has to remember is to be sure to thoroughly wash the knife used to slice gizzard shad, so that no trace of odor will be transferred to other fish cut with the same knife.

Hirame Flounder

Hirame flounder is a fish with a migratory eye. Its right eye is in the usual place when it is young, but as it gets older, the eye moves slowly to the left side of the head. It lies flat on the bottom of the sea during the daytime, eyes upward, and camouflages itself with a protective coloring just like its surroundings.

Avoiding the frozen product, which is widely available, sushi shops make use only of the freshest *hirame*. Long considered the white fish *par excellence* for nigiri-zushi in the Tokyo region, *hirame* has a delicate flavor, which is greatly enhanced by a few drops of lemon juice or of a reduced sauce (*nikiri*) made by boiling together soy sauce and *mirin* (sweet cooking sake).

Gourmets favor the flesh running along the upper and lower sides next to the fins. Since these small strips are the only parts of *hirame* used for nigiri-zushi, this fish is expensive in sushi shops.

Hirame flounder

Suzuki, Sea Bass

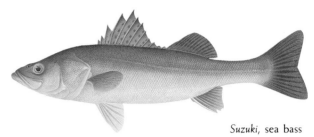

Suzuki, sea bass

In the distant past, a sea bass that lept into a fisherman's boat of its own accord was, not surprisingly, recognized as a great rarity portending good fortune.

A summer fish plentiful in all Japanese coastal waters from Hokkaido in the north to Kyushu in the south, *suzuki* (sea bass) was once ranked with sea bream (*tai*) as one of the finest of all fish.

Suzuki has to be the right size to be suitable for sushi. At 24 cm. (about 9 in.) it is called *seigo* and lives in rivers. The 30–40 cm. (12–16 in.) fish, called *fukko*, has moved to the sea, but not until it reaches 60 cm. (about 24 in.) is it called *suzuki* and used for nigiri-zushi.

There are many ways of preparing sea bass, and under various names several varieties are abundant in the waters around the United States.

To experience the taste of sushi
is to know the changing of the seasons.

Saba, Mackerel

The best time to catch mackerel is in the autumn. Fisherman look for a glistening on the sea caused by the surfacing of great shoals of mackerel, and, indeed, the image is one any Japanese would be familiar with. The plump *saba* of this season are the most delicious.

Before modern transportation, Kyoto was too far inland to be blessed with truly excellent fresh seafoods. Perhaps for this reason, Kyotoites devised ways to preserve mackerel, plentiful in all Japanese waters, for sushi. It was in the pressed sushi called *battera* that it became popular in that area.

Though today readily available in fresh form in those days *saba* was always salted for overland travel to Kyoto from the Japan Sea. And skill in salting spelled success or failure for the fish as food. Since it spoils easily, mackerel is often vinegar-marinated, though today it is used fresh as well.

Saba, mackerel

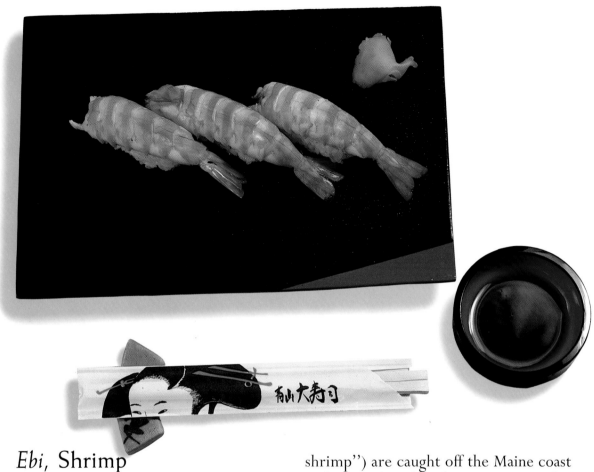

Ebi, Shrimp

Beautiful in color, delicate in flavor, shrimp is indispensable to nigiri-zushi, and of the many kinds the one most often enjoyed is *kuruma-ebi*, or "wheel shrimp."

Ideally, fresh shrimp taken from their natural habitat—not those raised on shrimp farms for human consumption—are to be preferred, but with the present large demand for them, it is not always possible to insist on such luxury. Today the imported frozen shrimp reigns supreme in Japan. In America excellent shrimp of the kind called *ama-ebi* ("sweet shrimp") are caught off the Maine coast and are at their best between November and March.

For nigiri-zushi, shrimp are threaded on bamboo skewers to prevent curling, lightly boiled in salted water, shelled, deveined, cut open and spread. The shell of the tail fan only is left attached. (See p. 64.) Most sushi shops use *wasabi* horseradish with shrimp sushi, but either a light salting or a coating of a vinegar-sugar marinade is delicious too.

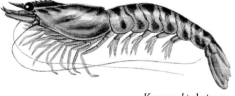

Kuruma-ebi shrimp

37

From the left are *nigiri-zushi* made with *ika; gunkan-maki* made with *ikura* and decorated with *wasabi* and cucumber to resemble tortoises, which are symbols of longevity; *gunkan-maki* made with *uni;* and *tako nigiri-zushi.*

Tako, Octopus

Madako octopus

Of the many varieties of *tako*, sushi shops prefer the common one known as *madako*, from the seas near Japan. Still, frozen octopus from waters off the shores of Africa are used too.

Octopuses are first boiled and then sliced for sushi topping. Though the body is sometimes eaten, the legs are much more popular. The underside of each slice of octopus must be scored with a knife to help it keep its place on top of the sushi rice.

Uni, Sea Urchin Roe

Only the very freshest *uni* (sea urchin) roe can be used in sushi, which, because of the nature of the topping, must be held in place with *nori* seaweed in the so-called battleship wrap.

Sea urchin are gathered off the shores of California for export to Japan.

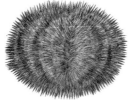

Uni, sea urchin

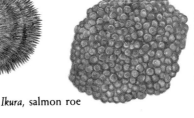

Ikura, salmon roe

Ika, Squid

Ika, squid

Tokyoites learned to use raw *ika* in nigiri-zushi after the disastrous Great Kanto Earthquake of 1923. Two older ways of preparing squid for sushi in Tokyo were boiling in soy sauce and sugar, or marinating in a sugar-vinegar mixture after boiling in plain water. Of the various kinds of squid, the ones called *maika*, *surume ika* and *yari ika* are the most favored for sushi topping.

Ikura, Red Salmon Roe

The Japanese word, *ikura*, for this delicacy derives from the Russian *ikra*, which means fish roe or caviar in general. From the standpoint of the preservation of species, consumption of salmon roe is perhaps regrettable. Nonetheless, there is no denying the meltingly delicious experience of salmon roe sushi, a favorite with a great many people.

Alaskan salmon roe is brought to Japan and reexported to the United States. As a rule, salmon itself is never eaten raw, due to the parasites that burrow into the subcutaneous flesh, thought it is safe to eat it salted.

Anago, Eel

Anago, common Japanese conger eel

Anago eels are found lurking in rocky crevices or buried in the sandy bottom with only their heads jutting out in almost all Japanese coastal waters.

Like that of gizzard shad, preparation of sea eel is a sign of the sushi shop's skill. *Anago* eel, indeed, presents even more of a challenge. After being boiled in seasoned stock, the eels are usually lightly brushed with a thick boiled mixture (*tsume*) of soy sauce, sugar and stock before being placed on the sushi rice. *Wasabi* is not used with *anago* sushi. Sometimes these eels are steamed and lightly grilled prior to serving. Many sushi shops have their own *anago* specialities.

Sushi shops in the United States sometimes coat the delicious upper and lower strips of *hirame* flounder in *tsume* and substitute it for *anago*.

Awabi, Abalone

Awabi, abalone

Awabi is best in April, May and June, and the opening day for divers to begin taking this shellfish is fixed as April 1. It is always found in rocky underwater areas near the *kombu* and *nori* seaweeds on which it feeds. The divers pry the abalone from the rocks with a forked metal rod.

In the days before World War II, the flesh of this marine univalve mollusk was always steamed in salt water before it was used as a sushi topping. Today, however, it appears uncooked, in spite of the fact that its toughness makes it hard on people with weak teeth. Most sushi shops serve only the firmer flesh of living male *awabi*, which is expensive. Sushi gourmets are especially fond of this topping.

In the United States abalone is found in the waters off the West Coast.

Akagai, Ark Shell

The monarch of sushi shellfish, the ark shell is a ribbed clam and has red flesh and, due to the presence of hemoglobin, red body juices. Some 8 cm. (about 3 1/4 in.) across, from the hinged side to the opposite side, it lives near the fresh waters at the mouths of rivers. It is best in the spring.

The flesh of the *akagai* is usually washed in vinegar to rinse away any odor before being used as a topping particularly attractive for its crispness.

Connoisseurs greatly prize certain inner organs, such as the *hashira* (adductor muscle) and the threadlike filaments known as *himo*, which together connect the flesh to the shell.

Shellfish are an excellent source of vitamins. The ark shell is especially rich in Vitamin A, B_1 and B_2.

Akagai, ark shell

Bakagai, Round Clam

Scientists call this creature *bakagai*—
"fool shellfish"—a name said to derive
from the foolish appearance of this
round clam in the sea when its red foot
projects from its shell like the lolling
tongue of an idiot. Sushi chefs would
feel awkward saying to their customers,
"Here's your *bakagai*," so they solve the
problem by referring to it as *aoyagi*, a
term traceable to the name of a town in
Chiba Prefecture east of Tokyo. It is
about the same size as the ark shell, 8
cm. across the shell.

Formerly, *aoyagi* was always lightly
boiled before being used in sushi. Today

it is often served raw. The adductor
muscle, which opens the shell, is as
delicious as the body flesh and is, in
fact, an expensive delicacy served in the
battleship-wrap style.

American sushi shops sometimes
substitute raw bay scallops for these
shellfish.

Bakagai, round clam

Torigai, Cockle

Torigai, cockle

The beautiful *torigai* (cockle), which measures about 10 cm. (4 in.) across, is found in shallow waters in most Japanese coastal areas. It is good anytime from August through April and is a true gourmet's delight.

The muscular foot of this marine bivalve mollusk is prized for its tenderness. This dark end of the flesh is said to resemble a chicken's beak and the taste is similar to chicken, hence the name, *torigai*, from *tori* (chicken) and *kai* (shellfish). To choose the best cockle for sushi, the shell is opened slightly to see if the flesh is thick and the foot dark in color.

An especially tasty and versatile delicacy, *torigai* is one of the two ingredients characteristically included in traditional Edomae *chirashi-zushi*, the other being shrimp. It also goes very well as an accompaniment to sake after being dipped in a mixture of soy sauce, *miso* and sugar.

Hotategai, Scallop

Hotategai, scallop

The opening and closing of the shell that makes the scallop move is said to bring to mind the wavelike motion of a ship's sail—*ho*—and this is the source of the name in Japanese.

The best *hotategai* (scallops) in Japan are grown specifically for food in northern waters around Hokkaido and Aomori prefectures. It grows fast, about 3 cm. (1 1/4 in.) in the first year, reaches 7 cm. (2 3/4 in.) the second year and 12 cm. (4 1/2 in.) the third year.

The ivory-colored adductor muscle that opens the lovely fluted shell of this bivalve mollusk is the organ found in nigiri-zushi. It is large and is sliced to be used on several "fingers." Other parts of the *hotategai* appear in other styles of cooking.

Mirugai, Horse Clam

Mirugai, horse clam

The main body of this large marine bivalve mollusk is edible but watery and unappetizing. The tasty part is the long, muscular siphon, which juts above the ocean bottom like a chimney when the creature is healthy and the shell itself is buried in the sand. To free the *mirugai* (horse clam) from its dwelling place, a jet of air is blown out of a pump to loosen the sand around it.

The function of the siphon is to ingest water and nutrients and expel water. This is accomplished by the action of cilia inside the siphon. The tiny algae growing on the outside of the siphon are washed off before serving. Another common name for this clam is *mirukui,* a play on words about the shell's looking (*miru*) as if it were eating (*kui*) the green algae (*miru*) that grow attached to the shell itself.

The horse clam is taken from waters around many parts of Japan and is found in the sea off the shores of northwestern America.

Shako, Mantis Shrimp

Odd-looking relatives of shrimp and crab, mantis shrimp spawn in the summer, when the females carry roe on their undersides between their many legs. They grow to a length of 15 cm. (6 in.) and burrow into the sandy bottom where they live. They are found widely, from northern Hokkaido to southern Kyushu.

To make sushi, mantis shrimp are boiled in salt water after the shell is removed, then brushed with a thick mixture (*tsume*) of soy sauce, sugar and stock before being placed on the rice. *Shako* continue to be popular as a sushi topping, though they are no longer used in *tempura* as they once were.

While the English word *garage* has been adopted into Japanese (pronounced, *garēji*), the Japanese word for a place to keep a vehicle is *shako*, so punning sushi chefs have been known to call the mantis shrimp *garēji* and mean *shako*.

Kaiwarina, Nattō

For the sushi-loving vegetarian, sushi can be made with fresh tender vegetables, fresh (avocado) or preserved (plum) fruit or *nattō*, a kind of fermented soybean, and other foods.

The appearance in ordinary markets of the delicate, freshly sprouted stems and leaves of plants of the mustard family is a recent phenomenon, and their development as a sushi ingredient dates back only a few years. This kind of sushi is called *kaiwarina*, one example being *kaiwari daikon*, the sprouts of the giant white radish so common in Japan. The flavor is light and slightly astringent. And they are refreshingly crisp.

Wrapped sushi made with fermented soybeans is called *nattō-maki*. *Nattō* is a processed food made by bacterially fermenting soybeans and can be bought packaged in stores. It is most often eaten by adding soy sauce and mustard, stirring, and pouring the mixture on ordinary rice. In sushi it becomes the core of long, thin rolls wrapped in *nori*.

In the photo above, the top row is *nattō-maki*. The core of the second row of rolled sushi is plum and beefsteak plant. At lower right, between two pieces of *kaiwarina* is the very recently developed *tōfu* (bean curd) sushi. The *kaiwarina* topping is freshly sprouted beefsteak plant. The *tōfu* sushi has a thin layer of dried bonito dipped in soy sauce between the *tōfu* and the rice and is garnished with finely chopped chives and a dash of red pepper.

49

Nori-maki, Seaweed Roll

To make *nori-maki* the core material is placed on a bed of rice which is then rolled up in *nori* seaweed. (See p. 68.) It was created around 1820, though there had been a few kinds of rolled sushi prior to that. It probably appeared first in the elegant vegetarian cooking associated with Zen temples (*shōjin ryōri*). *Nori*-wrapped sushi may have been simply an improvisation, or it may have been made for the meals served after Buddhist wakes and funerals, when no fish was eaten.

Lots of things can be used in *nori-maki.* To say almost any food is only a slight exaggeration. Making this sushi is a good way to creatively use such varied ingredients as *shiitake* mushrooms and pickled plums.

This rolled sushi is either thick or thin. In Edomae-zushi the thick roll is preferred.

The photograph at right shows in the top two rows *kampyō-maki,* which is made with dried gourd strips. At the left of the middle rows is *tekka-maki,* containing red tuna flesh. The pieces with the green core are *kappa-maki,* made with sliced cucumber. These three kinds are typical *nori-maki.*

The fresh color and irregular shape of the core make *nori-maki* very appealing to the eye. Each piece is nicely bite-size and can be popped into the mouth easily, so it is a convenient food for picnics or other times when the hands might be a little soiled. The taste is light and simple.

Tamago-yaki, Omelet

The two kinds of *tamago-yaki* (omelet) are thick and thin. Both are used in sushi. (See p. 62.)

In the photograph below at lower left and lower right is thin omelet on rice. To fit it to the rice it is cut partway through lengthwise and folded downward. Since its shape is like that of a saddle, it goes by the name of *kurakake* (*kura* meaning saddle).

The thick sweetish omelet to left and right of the center in the photograph is often eaten at the end of a meal as a dessert. The way to ask for it is to say *ichinin-mae*, a term which can be used anywhere when ordering food. In a sushi shop it invariably brings forth thick omelet.

In Season

Seasonal changes are very important to the Japanese. No people on earth are more conscious of them, and their literature and culture as a whole are strongly colored by an awareness of the transition of time.

There was a time when the first foods of any season were ritually offered for the enjoyment of the imperial court. The word for these offerings was *shun*. At the present time the word occurs in a broader context; *shun* denotes agricultural and marine products when they are in season and at their peak of flavor, quality and abundance.

Some fish and shellfish are at peak condition when the females carry roe, others when fattened to endure the coming winter cold. In any case, there is no denying fish and shellfish for sushi are best, and usually cheapest, when in their natural season.

The following list indicates when typical sushi toppings can be expected to taste best in Japan (Tokyo) and on the northeast coast of the United States. In any country those who buy and sell fish will know when certain species are in season and will explain what and when to buy the varieties available locally.

TOKYO		NEW YORK	
Spring		**Spring**	
akagai	*kohada*	ark shell	sea urchin
awabi	*madai*	bonito	(from Maine)
bakagai	*maika* (mid spring	fluke	smelt
hamadai	to mid summer)	horse mackerel	soft-shell crab
himedai	*mebachi*	porgy	spear squid
hirame	*mirugai*	**Summer**	
katsuo (mid spring	*tako*	ark shell	porgy
to mid summer)	*torigai*	blue abalone	red abalone
Summer		blue-fin crab	sea bass
akagai	*mekajiki*	Boston tuna	sea urchin (from Calif.)
hotategai	*shako*	mackerel	stripped bass
ishidai	*suzuki*	Meiji tuna	
kiwada	*uni*	**Autumn**	
kuruma-ebi		Boston tuna	sea bass
Autumn		mackerel	sea urchin (from Calif.)
hotategai	*shake*	**Winter**	
kuruma-ebi	*surume ika*	herring	sea urchin
makajiki		littleneck clam	(from Maine)
Winter			sweet shrimp
maguro	*surume ika*		
mirugai	*tako*		
saba			

3. Sushi Making

Materials

Powdered *wasabi* comes in a variety of packages. The cans at top and at bottom center and the packages with designs are all *wasabi*. At right top is rice vinegar, at right bottom rice as it is sold in plastic bags.

1. *Kampyō* calabash strips. 2. *Shiitake* mushrooms. 3. *Nori* seaweed. 4. Powdered green tea (*sencha* grade). 5. *Nattō* (fermented soybeans). 6. *Gari* (pickled ginger root).

Utensils

1. *Hangiri* rice tub. 2. Stainless colander (*kome-agezaru*). 3. Wooden container for serving rice (*ohachi*). 4. Bamboo colander. 5. Chopping board. 6. Stainless mixing bowls. 7. Kitchen chopsticks. 8. Rice spatula. 9. Fish scaler. 10. Paper fan. 11. Bamboo rolling mats. (Sushi is this book is made with the larger one.) 12. Vegetable knife. 13. Large and small cleavers. 14. Blunt ended and pointed fish knives.

55

Materials, Utensils and Procedures

Having enjoyed sushi in a sushi shop, you may want to prepare this nutritious food at home. Before going into detailed instructions, let's take a look at the basic ingredients and the utensils that are required for making nigiri-zushi and maki-zushi.

Materials

RICE

The 3 factors spelling success or failure for nigiri-zushi are the topping, skill in hand-making the sushi, and the rice. Many people like to eat newly harvested rice, but for sushi, grain that has aged awhile is to be preferred. Sushi chefs who know their rice have their rice dealers mix grains of different stages of maturity and from various regions to meet their specific requirements.

Su, RICE VINEGAR

Only vinegar of the highest quality is suitable for sushi, and only rice vinegar is used, since it has a gentle tartness and leaves a pleasant aftertaste. In the United States, Mitsukan Vinegar, a product of Japan's largest manufacturer of this condiment, is readily available. The ways certain sushi shops make their own vinegar are, of course, professional secrets.

Wasabi, JAPANESE HORSERADISH

Though the word "horseradish" has come to be used in connection with *wasabi*, the plants from which it and Western horseradish are made are different.

Nose-tinglingly sharp *wasabi* is especially good when the root is just freshly grated, but this is not always practical when large quantities are needed. Powdered *wasabi*, like the excellent seasoning sold under the brand names Kaneku and Kin-jirushi, is sold in cans. (Both brands are available in America.) Powdered *wasabi* must be mixed with a small amount of tepid water and allowed to stand for about 10 minutes before use. *Wasabi* is also made into a paste and sold in tubes.

Murasaki, SOY SAUCE

Shōyu, as it is usually called, is absolutely essential to traditional Japanese food. It comes in dark and light varieties. The dark kind is used for sushi.

Gari, PICKLED GINGER

A small quantity of *gari* is made by thoroughly washing and salting 225 g. (1/2 lb.) of fresh ginger root. After letting it stand for a day, it is washed again and placed in a marinade made of 1 cup rice vinegar, 7 Tbsps water and 2 1/2 tsps sugar. Allow the ginger to marinate for 1 week. It will turn pink.

Drained, covered and refrigerated, *gari* will keep for months. It is sliced thin to be served with sushi.

Nori SEAWEED

Nori is specifically Porphyra, a genus of red marine algae. After harvesting, it is dried, toasted and sold packaged in standard size sheets (19×21 cm., 7 1/2 by 8 1/4 in.), often folded in half lengthwise with the smoother side out. Once the sealed cellophane or plastic bag has been opened, *nori* should be eaten at once. If not, it should be stored in a sealed container in a dark, cool, dry place to preserve its crispness.

Toasting lightly enhances the flavor. If only untoasted *nori* is available or if opened *nori* becomes damp, pass one side over an open flame. Applying heat to both sides reduces aroma and flavor. In selecting *nori* aroma, color and luster are major considerations.

Ocha, TEA

The tea drunk with Japanese style meals is "green" tea, green being the color of the leaves, which are steamed after picking. If not steamed, the leaves ferment and become the black tea leaves customarily brewed for Western tea. Nothing is ever added to *ocha*.

To prepare green tea at home, leaf tea, rather than powdered tea, is preferred. There are many grades of green tea. For sushi, *bancha*, the least expensive, or *sencha*, a medium grade, are recommended.

Brewing green tea is not difficult. Hot water is first poured into the teapot to warm it, then discarded. For *bancha*, boiling water is added to leaves placed in the teapot. Allow to steep for 2 or 3 minutes. For *sencha*, the water should not be boiling; 80°C. (175°F) is ideal. Steep for 1 minute. Tea should be poured as soon as it is ready.

Utensils

The following are the utensils necessary to the preparation of sushi, though substitutions are possible and sometimes unavoidable. The ordinary utensils and vessels found in a well-equipped kitchen are used too, of course.

Hangiri, RICE-COOLING TUB

Made of *sawara* cypress bound with copper hoops, the low-sided, broad *hangiri* is perfect for cooling vinegared sushi rice and giving it the proper texture and gloss. Any suitable wooden, plastic or enameled vessel of the right size may be substituted.

Shamoji, SPATULA

The flat, round-ended rice-serving spatula called *shamoji* is traditionally made of wood and is a symbol of the housewife's position in the household. It is used to turn and spread sushi rice while cooling it. Some people object to the slightly woody flavor the spatula may impart to the rice and use *shamoji* of Bakelite instead. A large wooden spoon will serve in place of the *shamoji*.

Uchiwa FAN

This type of fan comes in handy to drive off moisture and encourage evaporation, which is vital to getting the right texture and flavor of sushi rice. The *uchiwa* is a flat fan made of bamboo ribs covered with either paper or silk. If no fan is available, a piece of heavy paper or cardboard will do the job.

Zaru, COLANDER

Now made largely of metal or plastic, the traditional Japanese bamboo colander was often a utensil of great functional beauty. It is used in washing and draining rice and other ingredients. The metal colander specifically for draining rice is called *kome*-(uncooked rice) *agezaru*.

Manaita, CHOPPING BOARD

This used always to be made of wood, but today for various reasons, such as hygiene, chopping boards of rubber or resin are common. The wooden *manaita* is still convenient, especially for pinning and holding eels in place while skinning them.

KNIVES

Serrated stainless-steel knives cannot be used in making sushi. They tear instead of cutting clean, leaving rough edges and spoiling the appearance of the finished food. The only way to be sure of ending up with nicely cut surfaces is to have steel knives of good quality and whetstones, and sharpen the blades yourself. An electric knife sharpener will not do the job properly. Good Japanese knives are an outgrowth of forging the world-famous Japanese sword. Cooks in Japan care tenderly for their knives, which they count among their most prized possessions. The following types are nice to have when making most Japanese foods.

Deba-bōchō (cleavers) are wide heavy knives with a triangular-shaped blade capable of cutting bone. They are primarily fish knives and come in several sizes.

Nakiri-bōchō (vegetable knives) are lighter than cleavers and the blade is rectangular in shape, but the back of the blade is sometimes rounded at the end.

Sashimi-bōchō (fish knives) are long and slender. The pointed type, most popular in Osaka, is called *yanagi-ba*, or willow-leaf blade. The blunt-ended type, most popular in Tokyo, is called *tako-biki bōchō*, or octopus knife. Excellent for filleting and slicing fish, they are also just right for such things as slicing rolled sushi.

Sushi chefs keep a folded wet cloth close by, frequently wiping the blades to keep their knives clean as they work.

Uroko otoshi, FISH SCALER

To clean and prepare fish at home, a fish scaler is best. The back edge of a cleaver can also be used for this purpose.

Saibashi, CHOPSTICKS

Once accustomed to them, many people wonder how they ever did without kitchen chopsticks. They are 2 to 3 times longer than ordinary chopsticks and permit one-handed manipulation of all kinds of food.

Makisu, BAMBOO MAT

This simple mat, made of slender strips of bamboo woven together with cotton string, is essential for the preparation of many kinds of rolled sushi.

Procedures

To Make Sushi Rice

To make good sushi, the rice must be cooked in the right way.

INGREDIENTS

Rice

3 1/3 cups short-grain rice

4 cups water

Vinegar mixture

5 Tbsps plus 1 tsp rice vinegar

5 Tbsps sugar

4 tsps salt

1.   Wash the rice until the wash water runs clean and drain in a colander for 1 hour.

2.   Place the drained rice in a rice cooker or in a pot with a close-fitting lid and add water. Cover and bring the water to a boil over a medium heat.

3.   Cover tightly and boil over high heat for 2 minutes. Reduce heat to medium and boil for another 5 minutes.

4.   Over a low heat, cook for 15 minutes, or until all the water has been absorbed.

5.   Remove from heat. Take off the lid, spread a clean kitchen towel over the top of the pot, replace the lid and let stand for 10 to 15 minutes.

6.   While the rice is cooking, combine the vinegar ingredients in an enamel bowl and heat slowly till the sugar has dissolved, stirring constantly. Remove from heat. To cool quickly, place the enamel bowl in a bowl of ice cubes.

7.   Empty the rice into a *hangiri* (or other nonmetallic) tub and spread it evenly over the bottom with a *shamoji* or a large wooden spoon. Run the spatula through the rice in right-and-left slicing motions to separate the grains. As you do this, slowly add the vinegar mixture. You may not need all of it. Avoid adding too much; the rice must not be mushy.

8.   Continue the slicing motions with the spatula as you add the vinegar. All the while you do this, have a helper fan the rice with a fan (*uchiwa*) or a piece of cardboard.

9.   The fanning and mixing take about 10 minutes, that is, until the rice reaches room temperature. Do not refrigerate the rice, but keep it in the tub, covered with a clean cloth, until you are ready to use it. Sushi rice lasts only one day and does not lend itself to the usual ways of dealing with leftovers.

Place cooked rice in *hangiri* and spread evenly.

Add vinegar mixture.

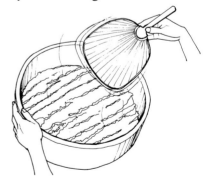

Fan to cool while mixing.

To Fillet Sea Bass

The fish shown here is *suzuki* (sea bass). The filleting of other fish is similar in method.

Always wet and wipe the chopping board before starting. The knives used are the *deba-bōchō* and *sashimi-bōchō*. Keep a clean damp cloth handy for wiping the knives and the board.

1. Scale and wash the fish thoroughly.
2. Place the fish on the board. Holding it firmly with one hand, use the tip of the cleaver (*deba-bōchō*) to sever the small bones at the bases of the gills on both sides. Remove the gills from both sides.
3. With the fish on its side, head to the right, make an incision in the belly from the pelvic fin to the anal orifice.
4. Remove all the viscera with your hands. Then, running the point of the cleaver along the spine, free all blood pockets. Cut off the double skin at the belly.
5. Wash the visceral cavity under running water, and with a stiff brush or a bamboo whisk, carefully scrub out all the remaining blood.
6. Return the fish to the board and

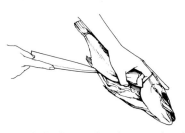

Remove gills.

Cut off double skin at belly.

Cut belly from pelvic fin to anal orifice.

Cut gills and back of neck.

Remove viscera.

Cut belly side from head to tail.

cut the gills toward the head and the back of the neck toward the head on both sides.

7. With the head of the fish to the right, cut along the belly side from the gill slits. The knife tip should extend only as far as the spine. After cutting through the bones at the edge of the visceral cavity, continue to cut toward the tail. Only the lightest pressure is applied. The knife, which must be very sharp, does the work.

8. Turn the fish so the head is to the left. With the knife tip going only as far as the spine, cut from tail to head.

Cut off the first fillet by letting the knife go all the way through and slicing from head to tail.

9. Turn the fish over and cut the head off.

10. Turn the fish end for end and remove the second fillet by cutting first from head to tail (knife tip as far as the spine) and then from tail to head, knife going all the way through. (Quite a bit of flesh will still adhere to head and skeleton. They can be used in making stock.)

11. All remaining small bones around the visceral cavity are trimmed away.

Cut from tail to head.

Cut off second fillet from tail to head.

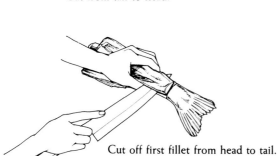

Cut off first fillet from head to tail.

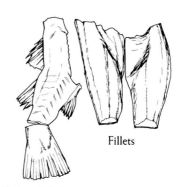

Fillets

Tail and skeleton

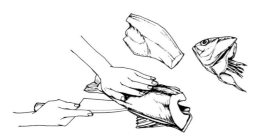

Cut other side from head to tail.

The very smallest must be plucked out with tweezers.

12.   The fillets are now ready to be cut into strips by slicing down the center (where the spine was). After doing this, place one strip skin side down on the chopping board with the tail to the left.

13.   Holding the tail firmly in your left hand, insert the blade of the fish knife (*sashimi-bōchō*) between skin and flesh.

14.   Keeping the knife at a slight angle with your right hand, pull skin and flesh in a gentle sawing motion with your left hand. The knife itself does not move. Keep it steady and let it separate skin and flesh.

15.   Repeat the process with the other strip. Then cut and skin the other fillet.

There are now 4 perfectly prepared strips of sea bass, ready to be cut into slices for sushi topping. Refrigerate until needed.

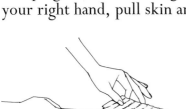

Trim off small bones.

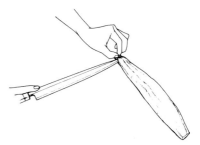

Insert blade between skin and flesh.

Slice fillet along center line.

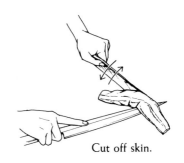

Cut off skin.

To Make Sushi Omelet

Thick sushi omelet is prepared in a large, deep, square frying pan, like the one shown in the illustration. The smaller, rectangular pan designed for domestic use will serve as well. If a square pan is unavailable, it is possible to use a large round frying pan by carefully trimming the omelet when it is set.

INGREDIENTS
   8 eggs
   2/3 cup stock or light chicken broth
   1/2 tsp salt
   1 Tbsp *mirin* (sweet cooking sake) or
      1 tsp sugar
   1 Tbsp light soy sauce
   vegetable oil for preparing pan

1.   Beat the eggs until whites and yolks are well mixed but not frothy.

2.   In a saucepan combine stock, salt,

mirin and soy sauce. If sugar is used, it must be dissolved by heating the mixture and then cooling to room temperature. Combine this mixture with the eggs.

3. Fill the square pan with oil and heat it till the oil is hot enough so that a small piece of bread dropped into it sinks to the bottom, rises at once and remains spinning on the surface. This step may be omitted if the pan is well-cured.

4. Pour out all the oil. Dip a cloth in the oil, fold it and keep it ready to reoil the pan during the cooking process.

5. Cover the bottom of the pan with a thin layer of egg mixture. Cook over a medium heat until the mixture is partly set and bubbly. With chopsticks, continue to break any bubbles that form, so that the finished omelet will be free of air pockets.

6. Run the chopsticks or a spatula around the edges of the egg layer to loosen it. Fold in 2 steps, reducing the area covered by the egg layer by 1/3, then by another 1/3. With the folded omelet in the end of the pan nearest you, oil the rest of the pan with the oil-impregnated cloth. Then slide the omelet to the other end of the pan. Oil the end of the pan nearest you.

7. Ladle in more egg mixture, and lifting up the cooked layer allow some of the mixture to flow under it. Again break the bubbles and fold when cooked.

8. Repeat the process until you have a supply of omelet at one end of the pan. Professionals adjust the shape of this, making a thick, firm block of omelet, with a special board. At home, the same result can be achieved by turning the omelet out on a bamboo mat,

wrapping the mat around it and molding the omelet to the desired shape. Allow to cool on a wooden board, and weight it with a flat plate so it will keep its shape.

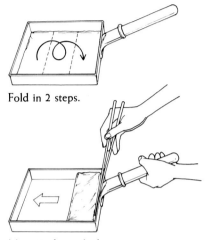

Fold in 2 steps.

Move to far end of pan.

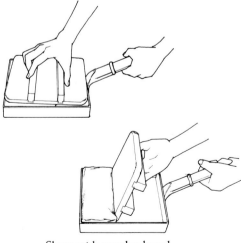

Lift omelet to let added mixture flow under it.

Shape with wooden board.

To Slice Sushi Topping

Cutting fresh fish into slices of uniform size and thickness appropriate for nigiri-zushi topping takes skill, which can be acquired with practice. The fish in the following case is *maguro* (tuna); the method for cutting other fillets is similar.

1. To measure the length, lay one hand on the block of tuna. The width of 4 fingers is just right. Cut this amount off the block.
2. Turn the cut-off block 90°.
3. Measure off 1 1/2 cm. (about 5/8 in.) from the left side. Using a *sashimi-bōchō* slice diagonally downward to the bottom corner to make a piece of flesh triangular in cross section.
4. To cut this triangular piece, lay it down with the side that was cut on the bottom. Placing the knife blade at the middle of the right side of the triangle, cut about two thirds of the way through the piece, then use the knife to unfold the piece. It is placed on the rice bottom side down to become the topping.
5. Continue to cut off slices by measuring off 8 mm. (about 5/16 in.) along the top and slicing at a slant to get pieces of uniform thickness. The last piece on the right will also be triangular in cross section and is cut to become topping in the same way as the first triangular piece.

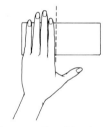

Measure off width of 4 fingers.

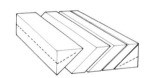

Cut into slices and 2 triangular pieces.

Cut triangular pieces into slices.

To Prepare Sushi Shrimp

Sushi-topping shrimp must be nicely colored, well shaped and opened flat to embrace the finger of sushi rice. Prepare them as follows and refrigerate until needed.

1. Before boiling, insert a bamboo skewer under the shell on the leg side of each shrimp to keep it from curling. The skewer should not pierce the flesh.
2. Boil in lightly salted water, just until the flesh changes color. Remove from the water, drain and remove the skewer.
3. Take off the head and shell but leave the fan-shaped tail attached. Using the point of a knife, trim off the small triangular segment of the shell above the tail without removing any flesh. This takes skill to do well.
4. Carefully make an incision along the leg side of the shrimp.
5. Deepen the incision so that the shrimp can be opened and flattened. Do not cut all the way through the flesh.

Insert bamboo skewer on leg side.

6. Devein the shrimp.
7. Lightly press the shrimp flat. It is now ready to be used for topping.

Remove head and shell but leave tail.

To Make Nigiri-zushi

The key to good nigiri-zushi is balance between the topping and the rice. It is hand-formed by gently squeezing the ingredients together. (*Nigiri* means "squeezing.") For one finger of sushi the topping weighs from 12 to 14 grams and the vinegared rice about 25 grams.

Before beginning the actual process, arrange on a buffet or serving table: a chopping board; a sharp knife (*sashimi-bōchō*); a clean, damp, folded cloth; a small bowl of *wasabi* horseradish; and a bowl of vinegared water in which to rinse the fingers. It is best to slice the topping from the fillets of fish as you go along, as is done in a sushi shop. The fish in the following example is tuna.

1. First pick up the topping between the left thumb and index and middle fingers of your left hand. Lay it along the base of the fingers of the left hand (not on the palm).
2. With your right hand, take the appropriate amount of rice from the container at your right side, hold it lightly and round it by tapping it gently and quickly two or three times on the inside of the container. The rice should be about the size and shape of a Ping-pong ball.
3. Holding the rice in your right palm, use the tip of your right index finger to place a dab of *wasabi* in the center of the topping.
4. Put the rice on top of this.
5. Lightly press the top of the rice with your left thumb, leaving a small depression on the upper surface. Keep the fingers of the left hand, and the topping, flat.

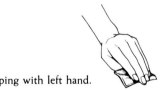

Pick up topping with left hand.

Press rice with left thumb.

Place *wasabi* in center of topping.

Press rice with right index and middle fingers.

6. Press the upper end of the rice with your left thumb while simultaneously pressing the bottom end with your right thumb.

7. With your right index and middle fingers, press the top of the rice, making the depression in the top more shallow.

8. Gently push the left upper corner of the sushi forward with your left thumb to turn the piece over. Slide the piece back to the base of the fingers.

9. Press the sides of the rice with your right thumb and middle finger. Then press the upper end with your left thumb, the lower end with your right thumb and the topping with your right index and middle fingers.

10. Taking the sushi between your right thumb, middle and index fingers, turn the piece of sushi around to the right.

11. Again press the top end with your left thumb, the bottom with your right thumb and the topping with your right index and middle fingers. After the topping is right side up, too much pressing will pack the rice too closely. One pressing, one turn and a second pressing are adequate.

Though the explanation sounds complicated in writing, once you go through the motions several times, you will become accustomed to and adept at them.

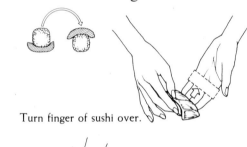

Turn finger of sushi over.

Press sides of rice with right thumb and middle finger.

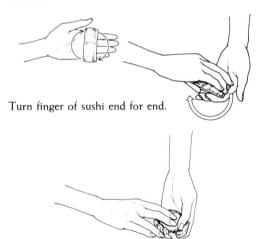

Turn finger of sushi end for end.

Press with right index and middle fingers.

To Make *Gunkan-maki*

As mentioned previously, certain ingredients, like sea urchin or salmon row, will not stay in place on an ordinary finger of rice. But the taste is too good to be missed, so the *gunkan-maki* was devised to hold such delicacies. It is made in the following way.

1. The same amount of rice as for nigiri-zushi (about the size of a Ping-pong ball) is formed into a mound.

2. A strip of *nori* seaweed long enough to encircle the mound of rice and wide enough to project 1 to 2 cm. (about 3/8 to 3/4 in.) above the top is wrapped around the rice. The rice is molded into an oval shape. The *nori* is held in place by crushing a grain of rice and using it like paste to fasten the ends together.

3.   With the fingers (not a metal spoon), place salmon roe in the bowllike receptacle formed by the rice and the *nori*. Place *wasabi* on top. A piece of cucumber cut in a fancy shape may be added for decoration.

Wrap *nori* around rice.   Paste ends together.   Add topping.

Nigiri-zushi Shapes

The fingers of rice for nigiri-zushi may have different shapes according to the amount of pressure applied when forming them and the way the fingers and thumbs are used. The following are the principal types, though the first two are not often seen at the present time.

Hako-gata: box shape. This is almost perfectly rectangular and requires considerable pressure from the fingers and thumbs. It cannot be successfully made if the rice is hard.

Tawara-gata: rice bale shape. Very little pressure is applied and the ends are not pressed with the thumbs. The shape is like that of the bales in which rice grain is stored.

Funa-gata: boat shape. This is long and rectangular, like the blunt-bowed Japanese boat.

Ōgi-gata: fan shape. This requires more pressure from the thumbs and less pressure from the fingers. It is rounded into the shape a folding fan takes when fully opened and is widely used today.

Kushi-gata: Comb shape. This is formed by pressing with the thumbs and with the middle and index fingers. The name derives from its resemblance to the ornamental combs worn in formal Japanese female hairdos. This form is the one most often used today. It is also called *Rikyū-gata*.

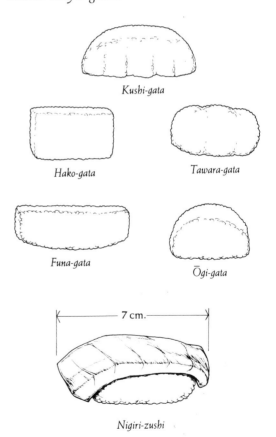

Kushi-gata

Hako-gata

Tawara-gata

Funa-gata

Ōgi-gata

— 7 cm. —

Nigiri-zushi

Maki-zushi, Rolled Sushi

Sushi made by rolling certain ingredients in *nori* seaweed with the aid of a small bamboo mat (*makisu*) and then cutting the rolls into slices is a great favorite in Japan. It is most enjoyable if eaten right after making, while the *nori* is still crisp, but if eaten later the same day it's still good. It is often found in lunch boxes or sold as a take-out at sushi counters in department and other stores. The two types are thin rolls (*hoso-maki*) and thick rolls (*futo-maki*).

Depending on the material used for the core, thin rolls are of three kinds: *tekka-maki*, made with tuna; *kappa-maki*, made with cucumber; and *kampyō-maki*, made with dried strips of bottle calabash.

Tekka-maki AND Kappa-maki
In the argot of the Japanese underworld a *tekka-ba* is a gambling den. The denizens of these establishments didn't like to get their fingers sticky when eating. But, like anybody else, they did get hungry. When they did, they ordered large quantities of rolled tuna sushi to be brought from the nearest sushi shop. In time this type of sushi came to be known as *tekka-maki*, but needless to say its popularity is by no means restricted to gamblers.

The story behind *kappa-maki* is that these cucumber rolls were named in honor of the mischievous *kappa* water sprite, who is said to be inordinately fond of this food.

These two thin rolls are made in the same way.

1.   Half a sheet of *nori* is spread on a bamboo rolling mat with about 1 cm. (3/8 in.) projecting beyond the nearer edge. In the middle of the *nori* arrange a band of sushi rice (about 70 gr.) from left to right. Leave the *nori* open (about 1 cm.) on either side of the rice and with your fingers make a groove along the center of the band of rice. In this groove lay strips of raw tuna for *tekka-maki* or strips of cucumber for *kappa-maki*. Distribute the fish or cucumber evenly and spread *wasabi* on top.

Kappa-maki or Tekka-maki

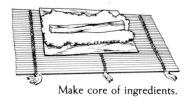

Make core of ingredients.

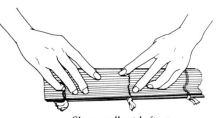

Shape roll with fingers.

Roll up in mat.

Cut into 6 pieces.

2. Starting at the edge closer to you, use the mat to roll up the sushi. After rolling, make the shape in cross section squarish by pressing the top with your fingers before removing the mat.

3. Take the roll out of the mat, cut the roll in half, then cut each of the halves into 3 equal pieces. Seen in cross section, the rice should be evenly distributed around the core.

Kampyō-maki, DRIED CALABASH STRIP ROLLS

Kampyō is sold packaged. Soften it by simmering for 20 minutes in a mixture of 1 1/2 cups stock, 4 Tbsps dark soy sauce and 1 tsp sugar. Then cool.

1. Spread half a sheet of *nori* on a bamboo rolling mat with about 1 cm. (3/8 in.) projecting from the nearer edge of the mat.

2. Lay a band of sushi rice lengthwise on top of the *nori* and, with your fingers, make a groove along the center of the band.

3. Fill the groove with *kampyō* strips.

4. Starting with the edge nearest you, use the mat to roll the sushi. While still in the mat, shape the rolls so that they form an arch. (The bottom is flat.)

5. Remove the roll from the mat and cut it in half. Cut each half in half again to make 4 pieces.

Kampyō-maki

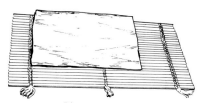
Place *nori* on mat.

Lay rice lengthwise on *nori*.

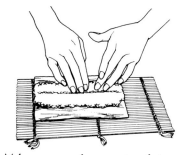
Make a groove down center of rice.

Place *kampyō* in groove.

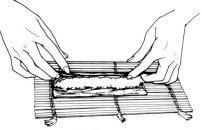
Roll up in mat.

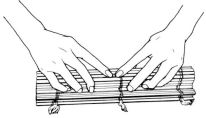
Shape roll to form arch.

69

Futo-maki, Thick Rolled Sushi

At one time these thick rolls of sushi rice combining a colorful variety of ingredients on the inside and a shiny sheet of *nori* seaweed on the outside were called *date-maki* (dandy rolls) because of their flashy appearance. (Times change. Mr. Ōmae calls his *futo-maki,* "Rock and Roll." Ed.) Needed for making them are sushi rice, chopping board and bamboo rolling mat, *nori* and a sharp knife. The following ingredients or any others that strike one's fancy may be included in the filling: raw tuna, thin omelet (cut in strips), cucumbers (cut in strips), *kampyō* gourd, *shiitake* mushrooms, *oboro* (white fish), *takenoko* (bamboo shoot), and *hasu* (lotus root). (See p. 69 regarding *kampyō.*) Mushrooms, *oboro,* bamboo shoot and lotus root are prepared as follows.

Shiitake mushrooms. Soften in lukewarm water. Trim, discarding stems, and slice fairly thin. Simmer for 15 minutes in a mixture of 1/2 cup stock, 3 Tbsps light soy sauce, 1 Tbsp sugar and 1 Tbsp *mirin* (sweet cooking sake). Allow to cool.

Oboro is sold bottled. If unavailable, prepare by first boiling white fish and removing skin and bones. Then squeeze fish tightly in a piece of cheesecloth or a kitchen towel. Grind the flesh in a mortar and add a small amount of red food coloring to make it pink. After combining small amounts of sugar, sake and salt in a saucepan, add the fish and cook over a medium heat until all the moisture has evaporated, stirring constantly with chopsticks or a fork.

Do not scorch the fish. *Oboro* should be fluffy and light, delicately colored and flavored.

Takenoko, boiled bamboo shoot, and *hasu,* raw lotus root, should be simmered for 20 minutes in a mixture of 1/2 cup rice vinegar, 1 1/2 Tbsps sugar, a dash of salt and 1/2 tsp soy sauce. Then allow to cool.

To make *futo-maki:*

1. On top of the chopping board spread half a sheet of *nori* seaweed. Add 1/4 sheet by pasting the edges together with crushed rice grains.

2. Leaving about 1 cm. (3/8 in.) on the right side of the *nori,* make an even layer of sushi rice about 1 cm. deep. Crush rice grains on the 2 right corners of the seaweed.

3. Turn the whole sheet 90°. Lengthwise on the rice lay bands of tuna, *kampyō, oboro,* lotus root, cucumber, omelet and mushroom. (Or bamboo shoot in place of lotus root.)

4. Rolling must be done with care. Starting with the edge closest to you, roll up the *nori.* Do this slowly, pressing with the hands to keep the ingredients in place. Fasten the corners that were pasted with crushed rice.

5. Use a bamboo mat to adjust the shape so that it is slightly oval. Slice by cutting the roll in half and then slicing each half into 4 equal parts. To ensure clean cutting, use a wet knife and wipe it after making each slice.

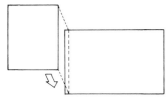

Paste ¹/₄ sheet of *nori* to half sheet.

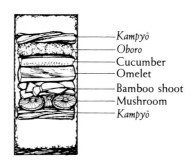

- *Kampyō*
- *Oboro*
- Cucumber
- Omelet
- Bamboo shoot
- Mushroom
- *Kampyō*

Spread rice in an even layer.

Roll up.

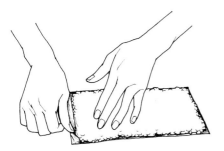

Leave 1 cm. on right side.

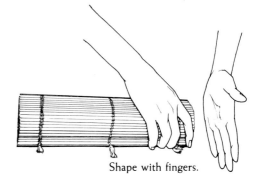

Shape with fingers.

Add *kampyō*.

5 cm.

Futo-maki

2.5 cm.

Kampyō-maki

2.5 cm.

Kappa-maki

71

Chirashi-zushi, Scattered Sushi

Chirashi-zushi means "scattered sushi," but this simple description does not adequately prepare one for this beautifully made and arranged dish.

In the Tokyo version, both cooked and uncooked seafoods, vegetables and omelet are "scattered" on top of sushi rice in a bowl. The bowl, often lacquered, may strike the eye as a work of art in itself. *Wasabi* horseradish is not used, but there is soy sauce in a small dish to dip the pieces of fish in as they are eaten.

In Osaka, *chirashi-zushi* is made by finely chopping the cooked ingredients— eel, fish, ginger, vegetables and so on— and mixing them with the rice. A little of the sweetened sauce in which the vegetables were cooked is poured on top, and the whole is topped with a layer of omelet. The omelet is made by beating eggs seasoned with soy sauce and a little sugar and cooking the mixture in a very thin layer, which is then rolled, cooled and cut into slender golden strips.

The Tokyo *chirashi-zushi* shown here features *chūtoro* tuna, yellowtail, sea eel, thick omelet, cucumber, grilled squid, shrimp, pickled bamboo shoot and cooked *shiitake* mushrooms. The secret is to put the vinegared rice (about 250 gr.) in the bowl gently. The rice should be only loosely packed. *Nori* seaweed, broken up into small pieces with the fingers, is sprinkled on top of the rice before other ingredients are added. Whether the cook is a beginner or a pro can be quickly known by how the final arrangement looks, as well as tastes.

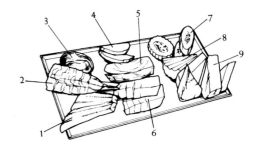

1. *Anago* eel. 2. Shrimp. 3. *Shiitake* mushrooms. 4. Bamboo shoot. 5. *Hamachi*. 6. *Chūtoro* tuna. 7. Cucumber. 8. Fried squid. 9. Thick omelet.

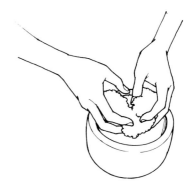

Place rice in bowl gently.

Sprinkle *nori* on rice.

Arrange ingredients on rice.

Party Sushi

Sushi of any kind makes a good party snack, but when you have a party, why not let your guests put together their own hand-rolled sushi?

To have everything ready, prepare Ping-pong-size balls of rice beforehand. Set these out on a serving table with the other ingredients. The only limit to these is ingenuity—tuna, shrimp, squid, shellfish and many other things are suitable if they have been prepared in the usual way and are ready to eat. A bowl of *wasabi* horseradish is essential, as well as a supply of half-sheets of *nori* seaweed. You will also need strips of *nori* 2 to 3 cm. (3/4 to 1 1/4 in.) wide. Have chopsticks and other utensils close at hand.

Each guest can hand-roll the sushi of his preference by one of the following methods.

1. Place half a sheet of *nori* diagonally in the palm of the left hand with the rougher side up.
2. Using a crushed grain of rice as paste, attach one end of a narrow strip of *nori* near the center of the sheet and let it project below the lower end of the sheet.
3. In the center of the sheet place a ball of sushi rice. This may be done with the fingers, but chopsticks keep fingers free of sticky grains.
4. After flattening and making a long groove in the rice, dab a little *wasabi* on it. Then add the filling or fillings of choice.
5. Make the roll by closing the hand and folding the *nori* over the rice and core.

6. The strip of *nori* at the bottom is folded up and held in place with the fingers. The sushi is ready to enjoy at once.

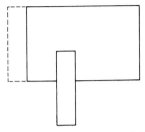

Place strip of *nori* near center of sheet.

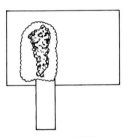

Add rice and filling.

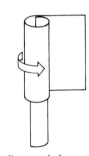

Roll up with fingers.

Temaki roll

If the ingredients are such things as salmon roe or sea urchin roe or *nattō*, instead of a simple roll, make the sushi cone-shaped.

1. Place a half-sheet of *nori* diagonally in the left hand.

2. Add the rice and filling as in the method above.

3. Fold the near corner over so it is a little below the center of the seaweed. Then close the fingers to form a cone. It may take a little practice to do this skillfully.

Temaki cone.

Place rice near left side of *nori*.

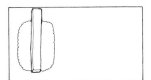

Place filling on rice.

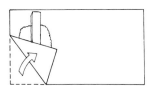

Fold near corner over.

The author (Mr. Ōmae) explains to foreign visitors how to make hand-rolled sushi using ingredients commonly found in occidental cooking.

74

Temaki-zushi (hand-rolled sushi) in cone shape.

Nigiri-zushi made with raw beef. *Wasabi* and sliced garlic are placed between rice and beef.

Sushi East and West

Many of the foods ordinarily associated only with Western cuisine harmonize astonishingly well with sushi rice. (For best results, when cooking the rice, use a half-and-half combination of rice vinegar and wine vinegar.) Try using marinated foods, thinly sliced roast beef, roast pork, ham, smoked salmon, chicken, tomatos or any other ingredient you think promising, as either topping for nigiri-zushi or filling for mat-rolled or hand-rolled sushi. You will find this hybrid "East-West" sushi can be expanded to include many new tempting treats suited to your family's tastes.

One tasty variation is the California roll, a slender mat-rolled sushi containing crab, avocado and cucumber. It is a great favorite in Los Angeles sushi shops, has spread to New York and is making a debut in Tokyo too. The creamy, rich, slightly oily avocado has something in common with the taste of fatty tuna. (It might be noted that avocados are delicious halved and served with a mixture of soy sauce and vinegar, or soy sauce spiced with *wasabi* horseradish, in the middle.)

Make the California roll by the method described on p. 74.

4. The Fish Market

Auctioning tuna, and a host of other seafoods, at Tsukiji begins at 5:40 in the morning.

The huge arc-shaped building in the foreground, near Tokyo Bay, is the Tokyo Central Wholesale Market at Tsukiji. It is about a 10-minute walk from the Ginza.

Buying and Selling Seafoods

Tsukiji

Tokyo has no shortage of wholesale fish markets; there are 73 of them in all. But the one everyone knows and the one most closely connected with the sushi trade is the Tokyo Central Wholesale Market, known as Tsukiji from the name of the district in which it is located. It is a huge and fascinating place, both in area and activity. The whole market, which also deals in agricultural produce, covers about 3 hectares (nearly 7 1/2 acres).Transactions in marine products alone annually run into hundreds of thousands of tons and involve billions of yen. Tsukiji is, in fact, the largest business enterprise of its kind in the world.

Fish has long been an important food and source of protein for the people of Japan, and for more than 3 centuries Tokyo's main fish market was located a little north of Tsukiji in the Nihonbashi district. There a family by the name of Moriichi set up business in the 17th century. The Moriichis were purveyors of seafood to Edo Castle, the seat of the Tokugawa shogunal government, but were permitted to sell on the open market after they had fulfilled their primary obligation. Gradually other fish dealers gathered in Nihonbashi, and the market flourished until 1923, when it was destroyed in the Great Kanto Earthquake.

Much of the capital was devastated, either by the earthquake or by the fires that swept the city in its aftermath, and the fish market was moved to Shiba, a little south of Tsukiji. It was during this period that laws pertaining to such facilities were promulgated and wholesale seafood markets began opening in major cities throughout the country. Work on the new Tsukiji market began in 1928; the formal ceremonies opening the market were held in 1933. At the present time, the people authorized to do business at Tsukiji comprise 7 major wholesale organizations, 1,226 dealers and 180 service organizations. During business hours, there is a constant flow of people; nearly 100,000 customers and visitors come and go every day.

Despite its size, this fish market resists being completely mechanized. In an age of computerized conveyor belts, goods are still hauled on carts pushed by women known as *chaya no bāsan* ("teahouse aunties"). They transport merchandise that has been sold and labeled for delivery by the dealers to the central shipping platform. The visitor won't see many young women among the *chaya no bāsan*, for they have to be made of stern stuff to cope with the rough-talking men who deal in fish. During the short trading session—about 4 1/2 hours—in this bustlingly busy arena, the *bāsan*'s chores may be complicated by errors, such as mislabeled goods or purchases sent (or not sent) to customers who didn't (or did) order them. Yet they accomplish a staggering amount of work each morning.

The central shipping platform in the heart of the market has its own rather surprising name: Shiomachijaya. This means, "Teahouse for Awaiting the Tide," and, whatever the realities of the surroundings, is evocative of swaying willows along the banks of the Sumida River in old Edo. In the area fanning out from the shipping platform are arranged the scores of stalls where dealers display their goods and conduct business. Dealers are divided into 3 categories. Some deal only in shrimp, others in large products and others in special products. Sushi shop proprietors go primarily to the dealers in special products.

In such a vast area, certain locations are obviously more desirable than others. To make sure that merchants do not monopolize the best spots indefinitely, lotteries to reassign locations are held every 3 years.

During the afternoon the streets around the Tsukiji market are not much different from those in many another district of the metropolis. Then the fish and shellfish begin arriving from all over the country. Some of the fishing fleets' catch comes by boat, as it must have for centuries, but today many products are brought by trucks, which rumble through the streets until about 3 o'clock in the morning.

About an hour later the major wholesalers look over the merchandise, assess the quality of the day's offerings and roughly set the prices they think they can expect.

At 5:40 A.M. a siren wails and the auctioneers begin their spiel. The buying and selling take place at 11 locations, each of which handles a specific kind of seafood. While the sellers carry on in a lingo that only fish dealers could understand, the buyers communicate with a full array of code signs. The pace is fast, and if any hitches impede the proceedings, they are resolved on the spot. This is often done by means of *janken*, the simple but fast game of paper-scissors-rock, and then the bidding goes on. Here again mechanization is not welcome. Computers were once introduced into the auctioning, but they proved to be unpopular and fell into immediate disuse.

Most of this phase of the trading is finished by 6:30, and the dealers have moved their purchases to their stalls and are ready to catch the eye of early buyers. Any buyer who wants the freshest seafood had better be on hand then. By 7 o'clock all the best quality merchandise is already sold.

Some people buy the number of fish they want. Others buy by weight, a practice which has been gaining in popularity recently. In any case buying fish requires skill and shrewdness.

Fish are kept in water, and the unwary buyer can end up paying for what comes out of the tap. Though the trick is rarely seen today, there was a time when an unscrupulous dealer who had spotted an inexperienced buyer would put squid on the scales with the tentacles up in the air. The water drained into the body, and the scales registered somewhat more than the weight of the squid. The buyer who was on to this would counter by picking each squid up by the head, emptying out the water and setting it on the scale trays himself. This gave him the added advantage of feeling the flesh, by which, if he were an expert, he could judge its freshness. He still had to be wary, though. The weight of the scale tray was included in the total weight. It was worth doing a little mental arithmetic on his own to be sure that the weight of the tray was deducted before the final price was marked on the squid.

Prolonged haggling over prices is not a national custom in Japan, as it is in some countries of the world. The men who work at the Tsukiji fish market are quick-witted and dislike procrastination and muddles of any sort. Any difficulty that arises is settled then and there, as fast as possible. Still it is a commodity market, and the dealers naturally want to dispose of their stock on the day of purchase. For buyers, this means that they can make the best deal by purchasing in large quantities. Even so, the reaction when they say, "I'll give you so much for the lot—and no more," will vary. If trading is brisk, the dealer will ignore such blandishments, but if things are moving slowly, he may very well say, "Sold! No time for bickering." To get a good bargain, the buyer has to be as sharp as the dealer.

The buyers at Tsukiji do not include retailers like the man at the neighborhood fish shop. The law forbids it, and he has to rely on the men above him in the chain of distribution. But the last days of December, when everyone in Japan likes to feel he has finished all the year's business, are an exception. Dealers are eager to clear their shelves before the long New Year holiday. The law gets bent a little, and Tsukiji is thronged with ordinary shoppers.

The people of Tokyo, or at least the natives, have long been known for an aversion to getting involved in complicated financial arrangements. So not surprisingly the rule at Tsukiji is cash on the barrelhead. Though nowadays the sums that change hands may be quite large and evidence of bank deposits or checks are becoming acceptable, the majority of Tsukiji dealers still prefer cash.

Large bankrolls are, of course, apt to attract pickpockets. Not so long ago the thief who got caught at Tsukiji quickly came to wish he hadn't. The dealers were inclined to take care of him promptly and none too gently. But this too has changed. Now there are special security guards and police boxes are strategically located. The treatment the thief receives will be stern but it's not likely to be violent.

On most days nothing unfortunate happens. Activity tapers off and by 11 A.M. nearly everything has been sold. By noon buyers are rare and the stalls are all closed down for the day. The 20,000 cars and trucks that packed the place earlier have vanished. Then comes the afternoon lull before freight starts arriving for the next day's trading.

Getting up early does something for the appetite, but no one need go away hungry. Restaurants selling food made from fresh ingredients abound in the vicinity. Within and just outside the market itself are eating and drinking stalls and, oddly enough, stalls selling great quantities of toys. All do a brisk business, both with the traders, who are in the habit of spending freely after finishing their business, and with the many visitors.

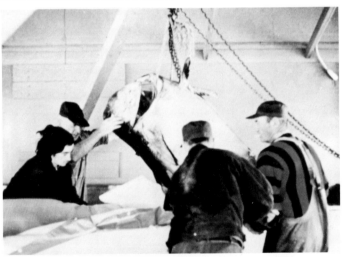

Some of Tsukiji's tuna are caught off Nova Scotia's Prince Edward Island. Ones weighing 300 kg., like the one below, are of average size. Head and tail are removed before they are loaded into the refrigerated containers in which they are shipped by air.

Uni caught by divers in the Pacific Ocean south of Los Angeles are opened to remove the roe.

How to Select Seafoods

What the sushi shop proprietor looks for in the fish he buys are basically 3 things. The eyes should be bright and clear, like those of a living healthy fish, not sunken, and the pupils should be black and unclouded. The flesh should be firm and springy to the touch. There should be no fishy odor, only the briny smell of seawater. In addition, if the gills are bright red, it is a good sign that the fish has been recently caught. Any blackness around the gills is unacceptable.

Tuna is sold already cut into large blocks, which should have clean firm lines. If they have begun to lose their shape, they are beyond their prime. When buying *katsuo* (bonito) and *saba* (mackerel), which are not good in summer, he will inspect the tail. The shape should be like that of the living fish. When bonito and mackerel get old, the tail droops. Shape is an important indication of freshness in *uni* (sea urchin roe) also, which loses its natural shape and firmness as it ages. For *tai* (sea bream) lustrous scales are desirable; the best size is 1.5 kilos (3 1/3 lbs.).

Imported shrimp are frozen. This is no handicap in certain styles of cooking, but for sushi, imported shrimp take second place to the domestic variety, which is sold live. The sushi chef looks for good color and lively movement. He will also buy live *ika* (squid), checking first to see that the suckers on the tentacles are still active. When it comes to shellfish, he will never buy any that are anything but living. If the shell of the *hotategai* (scallop), for example, is opened by hand, it will close by itself. Bivalve shells that are closed and stay closed are already dead.

Once the seafood is in hand, the question is: what part is the tastiest? As with birds and four-legged animals, the flesh of the fish involved in locomotion is the choicest. In most fish this turns out to be the dorsal side, but in tuna the fatty belly flesh is the first preference of sushi eaters. Similarly, the many legs of octopuses and squid are best, and, though there are exceptions, the adductor muscles and the foot of mollusks are the parts used in making nigiri-zushi.

Since a sushi shop's reputation depends on the quality of its seafood, the proprietor will take great care in buying. And he will often go to the hustling wholesale market place himself, rather than entrust the task to an employee. In the end, a discerning eye and sensitive fingers, which distinguish the novice from the professional, as well as adroitness in bargaining, are the result of experience and a willingness to study and learn.

5. The Chef's Training

The *Itamae-san*

To get to the top of his profession, that is, to become the master of his own shop, the *itamae-san*, the man behind the counter, spends a long time in training, often beginning in his mid teens.

Historically the *itamae-san* had something in common with the comedians of Edo. The growth of Edo dates from the beginning of the 17th century, when Tokugawa Ieyasu established his shogunate and he and his successors embarked on construction projects on a huge scale. His capital grew rapidly, people flocked to Edo from all over the country, and soon there were native-born Edoites. The typical Edoite turned out to be a lively brash, devil-may-care sort of fellow, though not without a certain charm.

Later, when a popular theater developed, the comedian was apt to greet his audience with a quip like, "Well, well. You must have a lot of time to kill if you can't find anything better to do than come here tonight."

The sushi maker, though he had no stage distance to protect him, could be even more sarcastic: "You don't like the way we do things? Out! We don't need customers like you." The only precaution he took was to soften the acerbity by expressing it in politely honorific language.

Such men were said to be hard drinkers. Some began imbibing in the morning and by evening were so far gone that business held no interest for them. They would match cups with their customers and still be eager to go out on the town after closing their shops.

In time another type of sushi chef came to be seen. He held his tongue, asking only, "What would you like next?" at the appropriate time, and drank not at all.

Nowadays, with shops selling Edomae-zushi located in all parts of the country and in other parts of the world as well, old ways have given way to new. Even stage comedians have to apologize, albeit grudgingly, for Edo sarcasm, and the sushi shop that fails on the score of courtesy is unlikely to succeed.

The young man aspiring to become an *itamae-san* spends the first 2 years of his training in a very predictable fashion—doing chores in the kitchen and, perhaps, delivering orders. His next goal is to learn how to cook rice. Japanese housewives who prepare this staple food daily probably could not meet the standards of the neighborhood sushi shop, where so much depends on rice being properly cooked. Judging such things as how dry the grain is, which determines how much water is needed, demands careful study. It is not unusual for 2 years to pass before the young cook can be certain his rice will come out perfect every time.

The next step is to learn the ins and outs of buying and preparing fish. This takes 3 or 4 years to become proficient at. By the time a sushi chef can be considered qualified to practice his art, he will have spent 7 or 8 years working and studying. He will also have obtained a license by having passed a stiff examination administered nationally by the Ministry of Health and Welfare. The ministry does not test technical proficiency—the customer rules on that—but it does determine that people who serve food are sufficiently knowledgeable about certain subjects, including hygiene, sanitation, nutrition and food quality.

The completion of the chef's training period is but the beginning of his career. As he goes along he is expected to master many things in addition to being able to make sushi.

He must speak well and correctly. This is especially important in Japanese, which has an elaborate system to express relationships, and courtesy, between people.

He must be able to manage the people working under him. For the sushi shop proprietor, at least, this means being involved in their personal as well as professional lives.

He must always be open to new ideas.

He must be punctual and never ask for time off without good reason.

If he drinks, he must be able to hold it well.

He must be immaculately clean.

He must be willing to work in the same shop for a long time.

He must have common sense.

He must know how to please customers.

He must wear neither a wristwatch nor glasses while working.

He must keep his hair cut short.

He must be clever and adroit.

Between a sushi shop of the first rank and one that does not belong in that category, the difference may very well lie in the skill and experience of the shop master.

One man who made it is Katsuo Niiyama. He was born in a mining town in Hokkaido. At the age of 6 he lost his father and had to help his mother take care of 3 younger brothers and sisters. When he was 13 he attended a memorial service for his father, and from that day on he had only one goal in life.

After the service, he went with other relatives to the town's only sushi shop. As he recalls it, the food was wonderful but even more impressive were the smart-looking young cooks. They wore polka-dot cloths of white and navy blue tied neatly around their foreheads. They went about their work with crisp efficiency. It seemed to Niiyama that here was real man's work, and he made up his mind then and there that that was what he wanted to do.

It was another 2 years before he could leave school, but after graduating from middle school, he went straight to Sapporo, the prefectural capital and the largest city on the island. He had taken the first step. He found work in a sushi shop.

One of his most vivid memories from

those days is of water and freezing hands. His workday began at 6 in the morning; in the wintertime it was still quite dark at that hour. His first task was to take buckets of water and rags and do the scrubbing. When that was finished, it was time to wash the rice. More water! He had to wash enough rice to supply 3 large pots 3 times each. "Anybody who doesn't like getting his hands wet," he says now, "shouldn't think of making a living in the sushi business."

Not a day went by when he didn't get his face slapped, perhaps for nibbling a bit of tuna or opening a pot that wasn't supposed to be opened, or perhaps for seemingly no reason at all. At times he was chased with a stick, and once he ran away. He was brought back and slapped around some more.

It was 3 years before he could begin to believe the hardest part was over and had gained enough confidence to go on with his career. He decided it was time to move on to Tokyo, the only place for a man wanting to study Edomai-zushi making to go.

"Just watch," he thought. "I'm going to work at a place in the Ginza. And I'm going to America."

His first job in Tokyo wasn't in the Ginza, however. It was in a sushi shop a little to the west in Shinjuku, a lively business and entertainment district. But he had to start all over from scratch. The same thing happened again when at the age of 20 he finally did make it to the Ginza. Since he was the most junior of 4 men in the shop, he started his third apprenticeship by serving tea.

Feeling it was impossible to train too much, he stuck with it. He gained confidence in his skill and after 2 years went on to another shop, also in the Ginza, where he was second in command.

Niiyama hadn't forgotten his dream of going to America. He managed to get a job with the Tokyo Kaikan Restaurant in Los Angeles and used his savings to make the trip.

Once there, he found life in a strange country anything but a bed of roses. He got homesick. He didn't speak English well, and this made him the constant butt of customers' jokes. Still, he wouldn't give up. He went to English classes to improve his linguistic ability, and little by little life became easier. Nisei residents and guests from the sushi bar started to invite him to their homes, treating him like a member of the family. He came to feel that Americans are generally open-minded people, and this helped him to deal with customers better.

Looking back, he says, "I suppose I was able to make it because I had a cheerful attitude and didn't worry or brood over things."

After 3 years in the United States, he felt he was ready for the challenge of having his own business. He returned to Japan and the sushi shop in the Ginza where he had been before. Then, while further honing his skills and knowledge, he looked around for a suitable opening.

The location he eventually chose was in a neighborhood where there were already 4 other sushi shops. But he took this to be a good sign. "If the local customers understand good sushi, my work will be easier," he thought.

Niiyama was then 28 years old. Three months before he was to open his shop, he got married. No honeymoon —in fact, no wedding ceremony. He was too busy with his work for that.

Once again he had to use up his savings, but this time they weren't enough. To launch his new business he had to make up the difference by borrowing from his family and a loan company.

He set the tone of his shop by giving it the name Sushiya no Kazoku, "Sushi Shop Family." He was making use of his experiences in Los Angeles and signifying his intention of making good sushi all the time and serving it in a friendly, family-style atmosphere.

Once under way, he brought all of his enthusiasm to this new venture. Rain or shine, he delivered orders himself. He never failed to send customers and acquaintances greeting cards at New Year's. When he was a youth in Hokkaido, no one there had heard of direct-mail advertising, but he didn't hesitate to use it. The reputation of his sushi shop, which is open from 11

After washing the entranceway to his shop, the sushi shop proprietor places small mounds of salt there, an act of purification like those found in Shintō, the indigenous Japanese religion.

Many sushi chefs visit Ōtori shrines, found throughout Japan, on a date in November corresponding to the Day of the Cock in the ancient lunar calendar. They bring back to their shops extravagantly decorated bamboo rakes. The mask in the center is called Okame, after a goddess, and there are sea bream, a gold piece and a tortoise signifying hopes of continuing good fortune and prosperity.

in the morning to·11 at night, spread. The number of customers has grown bigger, and Sushiya no Kazoku now serves about 560 men, women and children daily.

Niiyama has 3 full-time employees and 3 part-time helpers. The first thing he instructs his employees to do is to be courteous and relaxed. He then advises them never to lose their thirst for knowledge and improvement. He hasn't lost his, not has he stopped dreaming. He never stops thinking about new ways to serve his customers better.

Customers' Expectations

The sushi chef learns things by the number insofar as skills and materials are concerned. He must know many other things as well, since running a sushi shop necessitates continuous attention to both atmosphere and details. Among customers' expectations are these:

Consideration. No matter how good the food, a shop where the master is full of self-importance will not be popular.

A peaceful atmosphere. No employee should stare at a customer, or even look at him too long. Nor should he attempt to persuade customers to order what they do not want.

Stability. Frequent changes in shop employees would suggest variability in the quality of the food.

Quiet. A sushi shop can be a convivial place, but the chef should not talk while actually making sushi.

He can chat with his customers afterwards.

National Sushi Day

Sad to say, bad practices crept into the sushi trade after World War II. Prior to that only well-trained people ever dreamed of running a sushi shop. In the confusion of the postwar years, unskilled people got into the business end. They found that experienced sushi chefs were not easy to boss and needed little excuse to walk out of shops that were badly managed. When amateurs tried to take their place, they made sushi in a slipshod way, and the shop's employees suffered too, for they did not receive proper training.

Matters took a turn for the better after 1961. National Sushi Day was first observed in that year, initially for publicity, but it soon took on a more important meaning, namely to point out and, through contests, correct the sad state of technical ineptitude in many a so-called Edomae-zushi shop.

The contest began as a Tokyo event, attracted national attention, and at the competition held on February 24 and 25, 1981, the chefs selected to participate came from all over the country. Visitors were amazed at the virtuosity on display. Orthodox sushi traditions were much in evidence, but there were also new, pioneering techniques producing exquisitely beautiful and creative works of this culinary art. The world of Edomae-zushi never stands still, and any sushi chef worth his salt has to keep up with it.

6. Sushi Design

A Feast to the Eye

That eye-appealing food makes eating more pleasurable is undeniable. In Japan, it is not sufficient for food simply to satisfy the appetite. Texture and appearance are equally important. The cook who lacks a flair for making his offerings more than just presentable will not go far. This is especially true for the sushi chef.

The watchwords are balance and harmony in size, shape and color between the topping and rice of nigiri-zushi and the filling, rice and seaweed of maki-zushi.

Leaf Cutouts

The plant used to make cutouts is the aspidistra, a native of East Asia. Its richly green leaves are broad and stiff and only dexterity and imagination impose any limit on the elaboration of the design. Cutouts are used to separate different kinds of sushi when they are arranged in a combination set and for decorating fancy sushi.

Fancy Sushi

Sushi is not only everyday fare but a favorite for weddings, banquets and other special occasions. The decorative motifs may be floral patterns, the three plants traditionally thought of as auspicious—pine, bamboo and plum—the no less auspicious tortoise and crane, or any other design appropriate to the mood and the setting. Expert skill with the knife and a highly refined sense of color are the requisites of success. As a rule, the chef tests out his ideas beforehand to ensure that the desired effect will be achieved.

Noren

No sushi shop is without its *noren*, a short curtain hanging from about the level of the top of the door. When the *noren* is in place, it indicates the shop is open for business. When it's not, the shop is closed. These graceful curtains, often of striking design and incorporating the shop's logo, are a symbol of the shop's services and reputation.

Yunomi

One way the sushi shop impresses its customers is in the king- and queen-size teacups (*yunomi*) it provides them with. Ceramics is still a thriving industry in Japan, with well over 100 kiln centers producing wares of great functional beauty. The sushi shop proprietor specially orders his *yunomi* from a particular pottery. These teacups easily become objects of customers' admiration. To help people remember his shop—the shop name often appears on the cup, sometimes with the address and telephone number—a shop master will make a present of one of his handsome teacups to regular patrons.

Noren

Large *noren* like the one above are hung at shop entrances. The character in the middle reads, *"Sushi,"* and the ones at right (from top to bottom), *"Edomae."*

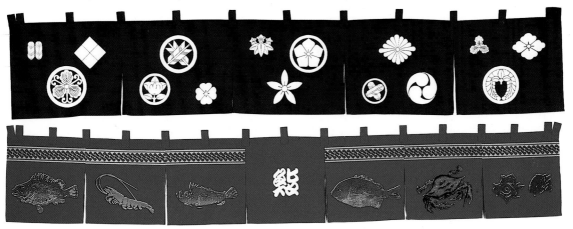

Smaller *noren* are used as hanging decorations above the counter or at other places inside the shop.

Cutouts

Carving aspidistra leaves into beautiful shapes to decorate his sushi is a skill the chef must master.

93

Fancy Sushi

The elegant sushi shown here was made with titles or famous scenes of Noh plays in mind and has been given the names (clockwise from upper left): Tō-bōsaku, Arashiyama, Tomoe and Miidera.

Left: Small sea bream and rice shaped like a mask.
Right: Peach made of omelet and plum.

Top: Boiled egg yolk suggests the moon. *Center*: Egg white and *anago*. *Right*: *Kohada* formed to look like the hanging log swung to ring a temple bell. *Left*: *Kisu* in the shape of a boat and ginger root.

Top: Sea bream and omelet form a cherry blossom. *Right*: Shintō wand, used in purification rites, made with ginger root, squid and trout.

Left: (Ichimatsu pattern) Omelet and mackerel on rice. *Top*: *Torigai* in the shape of a crown on trout. *Right*: *Ika* cut like a snowflake.

Food Models

Food models made of soft plastic look surprisingly realistic. Now found in all types of restaurants, they originated with sushi shops. The pieces of fish above are to be "eaten" as appetizers. At right is a combination set, a generous serving for 1 person (*ichinin-mae*).

Teacups

Every sushi shop wants to have its own distinctive *yunomi* teacups. The two at left bear the names of shops, the one in the middle a picture in the *ukiyo-e* style. On the two at right are written the names of sushi fish.

96

7. Nutrition

Health Food

The increasing popularity of sushi outside Japan is one indication of a trend. Today, for various reasons, people are becoming more cosmopolitan in their eating habits and learning that what they may not have cared for at one time can be not only appetizing but wholesome as well.

Traditional sushi ingredients fit in well with the modern preference for reducing intake of red meat and carbohydrates. To put it another way, not all epicurean delights are good for the health. But sushi is. As we have seen, canned or artificially preserved foods are shunned, and the variety of ingredients is astounding and satisfying. Aside from the fatty cuts of tuna, almost no sushi topping or filling is fatty, all are rich in proteins and some in minerals like calcium, phosphorus and iron. The vinegar added to sushi rice has antibacterial properties, prevents fatigue and lessens the risk of arteriosclerosis and high blood pressure. Shellfish are said to have rejuvenating effects on the body, particularly on the skin. Put simply, sushi is a health food in the truest sense.

Su, Vinegar

The observant sushi devotee soon notices that, despite the frequency with which they come in contact with water, sushi shop workers have soft smooth hands free of cracks or blemishes. The secret of this soft skin is the mild, protective acidity of vinegar, one of the most ancient of fermented products.

Sugared water or any alcoholic beverage, allowed to stand long enough, naturally sours and becomes vinegar. This can be seen in the word itself, which comes from the French *vin* and *aigre*, "wine" and "sour." Souring is the result of the action of bacteria in the air.

The kind of vinegar most widely used in any given nation is generally a clue to the kind of alcoholic beverage produced in the country. In Mexico, vinegar is made from cactus, as is tequilla. It is made from coconuts in Sri Lanka, a Buddhist nation where tippling is discouraged. In France, other parts of Europe and the United States wine and apple cider are common starting materials for vinegar. In Japan, it is made from rice, the grain from which sake is brewed.

Vinegar may be naturally fermented by bacteria-producing acetic acid or artificially produced by dissolving solidified acetic acid and mixing it with any of a number of additives.

There are many kinds of this fermented product, and flavor preferences change with time. At present in Japan, a fairly simple vinegar with a mild, light, slightly sweet flavor is the type used most often. Though other vinegars have their excellences and usefulness, there is no questioning the superiority of rice vinegar for sushi rice. The 6-percent proteins contained in rice are converted into amino acids during the fermentation process to give rice vinegar its distinctive qualities.

The wisdom of the people of the past, nurtured by experience alone, conceived in sushi a food that is remarkably safe in terms of bacteria, owing to the antibacterial actions of several of its ingredients. With the power to alter proteins, vinegar destroys bacteria, which are of course composed largely of protein. While it is true that dilution reduces its antiseptic powers, the strength of vinegar used in sushi rice is sufficient to do the job.

The following chart, based on experimentally derived information published in *Nihon Nogei Kagaku Kaishi* (vol. 10, 1934), a leading Japanese agricultural journal, by Professor S. Tetsumoto, shows the relative antibacterial powers of four sushi ingredients: *wasabi*, ginger, soy sauce and vinegar.

The things added to sushi rice alter the tartness, according to the temperature. Sweetness softens vinegar's acidity and enriches the flavor. For this reason, sushi rice, which is eaten cooled though not chilled, is seasoned lightly with sugar to prevent the tartness of vinegar from coming through too strongly. Care must be taken in adding salt, since the the lower the temperature of the food, the greater the seasoning effect of the salt. Though the balance between vinegar and salt seems perfect at body temperature, as sushi rice cools, saltiness can increase beyond the desired limit unless the quantity of salt is scrupulously gauged.

Shōyu, Soy Sauce

Because of the way it masks the rawness of fresh uncooked fish and harmonizes with such other ingredients as *nori* seaweed, soy sauce is indispensable to nigiri-zushi. Indeed, it could be said that without soy sauce, nigiri-zushi would probably never have reached its present state of development.

A researcher in Los Angeles has reported on the two favorite aromas of Americans; in order they are coffee and soy sauce. Interestingly enough this most oriental of all seasonings is produced in large quantities by the Kikkoman Company plant in Walworth, Wisconsin, using domestically grown soybeans.

Soy sauce is popular the world over, but this popularity was anticipated long ago. In the 16th century, Dutch seamen

	Cholera	Dysentery	Typhoid
Ginger	6–9 hrs.	30 mins.–2 hrs.	2–3 days
Soy Sauce	3–9 hrs.	2–4 hrs.	2–5 days
Vinegar	1–10 mins.	30 mins.	10 mins.–1 hr.
Wasabi	2–3 hrs.	————	9–12 hrs.

Time required for antibacterial action of sushi ingredients to be effective.

99

transported it from Japan through the Pacific and Indian oceans to Europe in bottles or jugs stoppered with wood, sealed with resin and sterilized with hot water. It found a place of dignity on the palatial tables of France during the reign of Louis XIV and has been enjoyed and praised by people in many parts of the world under many appellations: Japanese flavor, meat sauce, fancy food, all-purpose seasoning and so on. As mentioned before, Japanese soy sauce, rather than the darker and richer Chinese variety, is the one for sushi lovers.

Weight-watchers' clubs in the United States have included it on their lists of recommended foods and nutritionists regard it as a complete and rational use of soybeans. It is highly recommended as a natural fermented food, superior to salt, sugar or synthetic seasonings.

Due to the tenderizing effect of its enzymes and the slight amount of alcohol it contains, soy sauce is an excellent marinade for meats. The distinctive aroma and flavor of soy sauce are essential to most traditional Japanese foods, including sushi, *tempura*, sukiyaki and *soba* or *udon* noodles, though oddly enough nothing like modern soy sauce was made in Japan until the 14th century.

Dark soy sauce accounts for 85 percent of all that made in Japan today. The lighter variety accounts for about 11 percent and specially flavored types for the remaining 4 percent. Dark and light soy sauces are made in similar ways. Soybeans are steamed and combined with salt, crushed wheat and malt yeast to stimulate fermentation. This mixture is aged in tanks for one year. At this stage it already has the

distinctive soy sauce taste and aroma. Strained, this mixture becomes the dark soy sauce popular in Tokyo and the Kanto Plain area. In the Kyoto-Osaka area, slight alterations are made in the treatment of the materials, the yeast and the final preparations to yield a similar but lighter sauce, which seasons without overpowering the basic ingredients in broths, braised foods and casserole-style dishes. Still another variety of soy sauce is *tamari*. This is made of soybeans without additions of wheat and is dark with a thick, rich, slightly sweet flavor and a pronounced soy aroma.

A handful of large firms produce the great bulk of soy sauce sold in Japan and abroad today, though the actual number of firms is over three thousand. In choosing from the many brands available, the following guidelines should be helpful.

Aroma. No matter how deeply it is inhaled, good soy sauce never produces an unpleasant smell.

Color. When a small quantity is poured into a white dish, good soy sauce looks reddish.

Clarity. Good soy sauce is perfectly translucent. Sunlight passing through it gives it a lovely glow.

Soy sauce is heat-treated to sterilize it before bottling, but the richness of the nutrients in it will cause mold to form once the bottle is opened unless precautions are taken. While the mold is not necessarily harmful, it does affect the taste and destroy the aroma. To prevent this, opened soy sauce should be stored in a cool, dark, dry place or refrigerated.

Wasabi horseradish

Grown only in Japan, *wasabi* horseradish (*Wasabia japonica*), when grated fine, is a pungent, nose-tinglingly refreshing pulp that removes unpleasant fishiness. The glucoside sinigrin is responsible for the pungency of *wasabi*; it is activated by contact with oxygen when the root is ground, the finer the better. Because it volatilizes when eaten, *wasabi* stimulates the secretion of saliva and digestive juices, thus sharpening the appetite. It is rich in Vitamin C and has many times the antibacterial powers of ultraviolet rays. It may be that people of ancient times were wise enough to realize this and used *wasabi* as much for its antiseptic qualities as for its flavor.

Wasabi is difficult to cultivate. It requires just the right conditions, specifically the northern sides of shaded mountain valleys near cold running streams. Even when the environment is suitable, it takes 2 or 3 years for the edible roots to mature and even then they are not very large.

Fresh *wasabi* is understandably expensive, so it is also sold powdered and as a paste. (See p. 56.) Both are adequate alternatives and have the advantage of being reasonably priced, but of course they cannot rival fresh *wasabi* for flavor.

Gari, Ginger Root

In addition to being a fine mouth freshener, pickled ginger root has antibacterial powers too. There is even a legend about it. In the 17th century, during an uprising instigated by a man named Yui Shōsetsu (1605–51), poison was emptied into a river running through Edo and would have done great harm to the citizens of the shogunal capital had not a one-eyed old farmwoman been washing ginger roots in a tributary stream. The water in which the ginger was washed flowed into the contaminated river and neutralized the poison. Owing to this legend, ginger is revered at one of Tokyo's Shintō shrines, where a market selling ginger root is held periodically.

When purchasing ginger root, be absolutely certain to select firm knobs with smooth skin.

The ginger eaten in Japan is either imported from Taiwan or raised from stock introduced from Southeast Asia and now grown in Chiba, Kōchi and Nagasaki prefectures. Osaka sushi chefs like to flaunt their dexterity with the knife by slicing ginger into delicate julienne cuts, but this went out of fashion in Edomae-zushi in the early part of this century.

Nori seaweed

The first *nori* was cultivated in Tokyo Bay in the late 17th century. Since production was carried on in Tokyo's Asakusa district, it was called Asakusa *nori*. This seaweed is no longer grown in Tokyo Bay, but the nostalgic name Asakusa *nori* lingers on. Producing areas now are Akita, Ishikawa and other prefectures on the Japan Sea Coast and all prefectures on the Pacific Coast except Ibaraki and Tokyo, but about 40 percent is produced in one area, Ariake Bay in western Kyushu.

Nori's nutritional value lies in its protein, mineral salt and extremely high vitamin (A, B_1, B_2, B_6, Niacen and C) content. It is grown by mixing 20 species of Porphyra algae and cultivating the mixture in nitrogen-rich tidal seawater from November to April. Lack of rain, which provides nutrients, means either a small harvest or a harvest of poor quality. After it is harvested, it is washed in fresh water, dried on large frames, then cut into sheets and lightly roasted. The whole process is completely mechanized, and annual production comes to about 8 billion sheets.

All *nori* of the best quality is black. Since black *nori* is expensive, cheaper grades of green *nori* are marketed too. The green color is due to various other species of algae.

Calories and Vitamins

Sushi is a low-calorie, high-protein food with moderate amounts of carbohydrates and lots of vitamins. A 12- to 14-gram serving of fatty tuna has about 45 calories, salmon roe about 30 and *anago* eel about 26. Other toppings—the red flesh of tuna, squid, abalone, shrimp, bonito, sea bream and so on—have from 12 to 18 calories per 12 to 14 grams. Protein ranges from 1.4 g. (shrimp) to 3.1 g. (salmon roe) and carbohydrates from .1 g. (salmon roe) to .9 g. (abalone, shrimp and tuna) per one piece of nigiri-zushi. The vitamins commonly found in sushi seafoods are A, B_1, B_2, Niacin and, sometimes, D. *Anago* eel is a source of iron.

A typical sushi meal—a combination set of 7 to 9 pieces—has altogether approximately 300 calories.

Growing *nori* is work done in the cold winter months. At high tide the water reaches the level of the nets holding the *nori*.

8. History

Pickling and the Sushi Shop

The beginning of all sushi making was a method of pickling fish practiced first in Southeast Asia. Long ago the mountain people of that region preserved fish by packing it with rice. As it fermented the rice produced lactic acid, which pickled the fish and kept it from spoiling. It seems probable that it was during prehistoric times when this method of preservation was introduced to Japan along with rice cultivation.

One of the forms it eventually took was *nare-zushi*, a sushi made with carp in the vicinity of Lake Biwa in Shiga Prefecture. As had been the custom from the beginning, only the fish was eaten; the rice was discarded. The history of Biwa carp sushi, also called *funa-zushi*, is said to extend back 1300 years, and it is still eaten today.

Preparing *nare-zushi* takes from 2 months to more than a year. People in 15th and 16th century Japan came to think not only that this was too time-consuming but that it was a waste of rice. They were loathe to waste such a valuable grain, and this led in time to the development of *nama-nare* or *han-nare*, which matures in a few days. Eating both fish and rice dates from this period.

Arakan, or *rakan*, are Buddhist sages who through meditation and self-discipline have attained *satori* (enlightenment). The position of this Sushi-*rakan*'s hands is like that of a sushi chef making nigiri-zushi. Located in the garden of the Sōtō Zen temple Shōrinji in Yorii, Saitama Prefecture, the statue was carved between the years 1826 and 1832, not long after nigiri-zushi was created in Edo.

One thing the people of Edo were not noted for was their patience. In the middle of the 17th century, a doctor named Matsumoto Yoshiichi, who lived in Yotsuya, Edo, and was employed by the fourth Tokugawa shogun, Ietsuna (1641–80), hit upon the idea of adding vinegar to sushi rice. The resulting tartness was pleasing, and the time it was necessary to wait before eating the sushi was substantially reduced. Still, it was not eaten right away. In keeping with the culinary practices of the time, the rice and other ingredients were

boxed or rolled up before consumption.

It is the long association with pickling that gives the sushi maker's workplace its other name, *tsuke-ba*, literally, "pickling place."

By the early 19th century, the city of Edo was comparable in size and population to London, but Edoites still liked to get things done with the least practicable delay. After some trial and error, nigiri-zushi came into being. It is often referred to as Edomae-zushi, possibly (though the derivation is by no means certain) because the fish and shellfish used in it were taken from the waters of the large bay on which the city is situated. This gave Edoites an advantage over inhabitants in other regions. In the elegant cultural capital of Kyoto, for example, freshness in seafoods was a luxury seldom enjoyed.

Fish were usually preserved by salting or pickling or some other method.

In 1824 a man named Hanaya Yohei conceived of the idea of sliced, raw seafood at its freshest, served on small fingers of vinegared rice—an instant improvement on the other more venerable sushi dishes. The stall he opened in the bustling Ryōgoku district of Edo caught on at once, as this verse of the time indicates:

> Crowded together, weary with waiting,
> Customers squeeze their hands
> As Yohei squeezes sushi.

From a man who wrote under the unusual name of Sailcloth, we know that the squeezing methods of Yohei and his contemporaries were very much like the ones in use today. Sailcloth describes the sushi makers' hand position as *ninjutsu*, a term referring to a hand

Taking along a lunch of sushi when going on a flower-viewing excursion is an old custom. Scene above is from the *ukiyo-e* print, *Mitate Genji hana no en* by Kuniyoshi (1797–1862).

posture employed by the agile and ingenious spies known as *ninja*. It calls for the index and middle fingers of the right hand to be held in the palm of the left hand.

In old pictures the sushi shops of the Edo period (1603–1868) look very little like the ones of today. For one thing the cook worked seated behind a lattice. Still there is something familiar. A raised *tatami*-floored section for a small number of guests is shown in some pictures, and this might be considered the predecessor of the *tatami* areas in some modern sushi shops. And then as now sushi could be delivered, after a fashion. Men walked around selling it from large boxes carried on their backs.

A sushi shop in Tokyo around 1930. The stall, once on wheels, now forms the right side of the front of the shop. The young man with the bicycle delivered sushi to homes and offices.

In the middle of the 19th century, sushi stalls began emerging all over Edo. They were well patronized and endured until shortly after World War II. Many a proprietor of a splendid modern sushi shop got his start as a sushi stall operator. There were many ordinary sushi shops in the city too, but men with an independent turn of mind but a shortage of capital opted to purchase rights to operate stalls. The going rate for the rights varied according to the location of the stall, the most frequented spots being the most expensive. Since a popular spot enhanced the possibility of doing good business, prospective stall operators vied vigorously with one another to get the best rights.

The stalls had wheels and were hauled into place in the evening. Then the operator hung out his *noren* curtain to signify he was ready for business. One reason sushi makers did their work sitting down was to keep their feet dry. This continued even after the appearance of high-topped rubber boots in the 1920s.

Since stalls had no pumps of their own, obtaining water was a job in itself. The proprietor had to ask nearby householders for permission to fill several buckets. His initial supply had to last him all evening, so he was naturally careful about the way he used it. The bowl of water he kept for dipping his hands into grew murkier and murkier as the night progressed; it's doubtful that sanitation was up to today's standards.

He kept his wares in a box filled with ice, lifting the bamboo mat covering it to display what he had to offer. On the

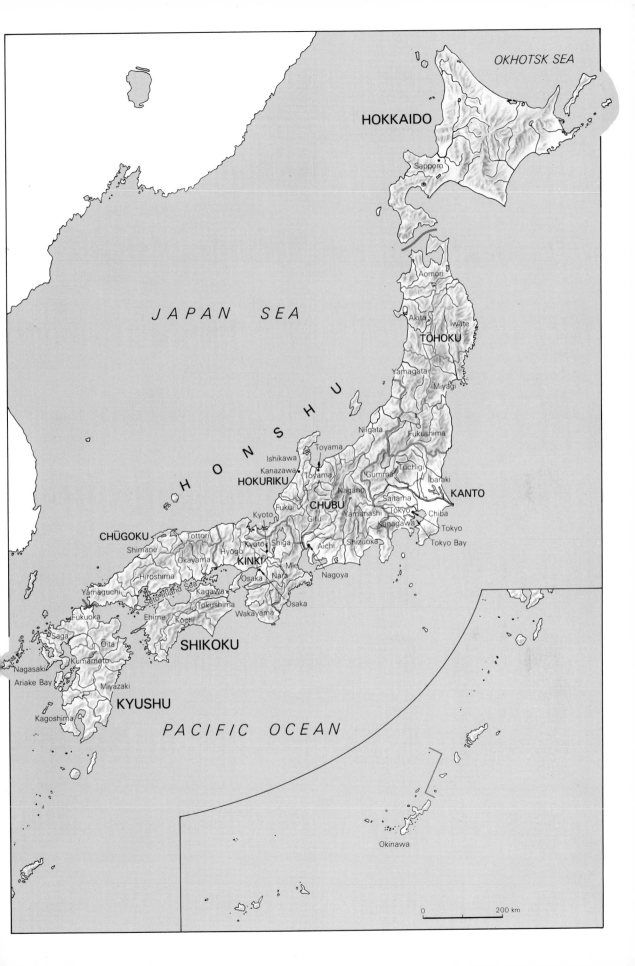

OKHOTSK SEA

HOKKAIDO

Sapporo

JAPAN SEA

HONSHU

Aomori

Akita
Iwate
TOHOKU

Yamagata
Miyagi

Niigata
Fukushima

Toyama
Ishikawa
Kanazawa
Toyama
HOKURIKU
Gumma
Tochigi
Nagano
Ibaraki
Fukui
CHUBU
Saitama
KANTO
Yamanashi
Tokyo
Kyoto
Gifu
Tokyo
Chiba
Shiga
Kanagawa
Tokyo
CHŪGOKU
Tottori
Kyoto
Aichi
Shizuoka
Tokyo Bay
Shimane
Hyogo
Mie
Okayama
KINKI
Nagoya
Hiroshima
Osaka
Nara
Kagawa
Yamaguchi
Inland Sea
Tokushima
Osaka
Fukuoka
Ehime
Kochi
Wakayama
Saga
SHIKOKU
Ōita
Nagasaki
Kumamoto
Ariake Bay
Miyazaki
KYUSHU

PACIFIC OCEAN

Kagoshima

Okinawa

0   200 km

stall's small counter, he set out one bowl of soy sauce and another of sliced pickled ginger. His sushi rice he cooked at home and brought with him in a wooden container. In winter the container was wrapped with straw so the rice would not get too cold and unappetizing.

The people who stopped by for a snack, for that is what nigiri-zushi was originally, might be returning from the public bathhouse or men out for the evening on business or pleasure. There was nothing very formal about table manners. Diners helped themselves to the ginger and dunked their sushi, sometimes fingers and all, into the bowl of soy sauce. Dirty fingers were no problem. The *noren* was right there to wipe them on. At the end of the evening, a well-stained *noren* was a good sign betokening a large number of customers —or a small number of very hungry ones.

The transition from sushi stall to the often elegant shop of today was gradual and began after the Great Kanto Earthquake of 1923. For a while after shops began to be built, the stall remained, parked in front of the shop. Customers who were so inclined purchased and consumed their food out of doors. The chairs inside the shop were mostly for the convenience of people waiting to have sushi packed in boxes to take out. Some sat neither inside nor outside but stood and ate at the front of the shop in an area which, though roofed, was fully open to the street. At this stage, the *noren* hung from a rod in front of the shop, rather than the stall.

Sushi stalls vanished from Tokyo streets forever after World War II, when Allied Occupation authorities decreed their demise. At first the stall was simply moved indoors to become the sushi chef's work space and counter. With this arrangement, customers could eat in comfort, no matter what the weather was like. There were no clouds of dust on windy days to worry about and having an adequate supply of water was no longer a problem, but certain practices of old stubbornly hung on. The communal bowls of soy sauce and ginger remained in use, the chef still sat down to do his work, and the customers stood up to eat what he prepared.

During the 1960s eating while standing up fell into disfavor in most types of eating establishments, though it was, and still is, all right to do so at festivals and markets. More recently, with the introduction of fast-food eateries from abroad, it has reappeared, but the customer in the sushi shop continues to enjoy his meal in seated ease.

9. Regional Variations

From North to South

A mountainous country surrounded by the sea, Japan has a climate ranging from subarctic in Hokkaido to subtropical in Kyushu and Okinawa. A great number of its flora and fauna are found nowhere else, and distinctive foods that complement regional lifestyles have evolved during the course of its long history. Many traditions and crafts have been preserved to the present day. While Edomae-zushi has spread all over the country, the traveler can take delight in local varieties of sushi too.

Hokkaido

Hokkaido was a virtual wilderness until the mid 19th century, when it was opened to intensive development.

Pioneers from all over the country learned to live in its harsh climate, and its dishes are a blend of the local cuisines they brought with them and adapted to local products. Good use is made of such Hokkaido specialties as herring, salmon and squid.

Tōhoku

Households are apt to be snow-bound during the long winters in the northern part of Honshu. For this reason, methods of preserving foodstuffs have reached a high level of sophistication in the Tōhoku region. To encourage the arrival of spring warmth, the people have created a sushi topped with fresh mountain herbs and plants.

I-zushi, a sushi made with fish preserved through yeast fermentation, has long been popular in Hokkaido. The fish used is *nishin,* a type of herring for which Hokkaido waters are famous.

Kanto and Chūbu

Tokyo, the focal point of the Kanto region, and Nagoya, the largest city in the Chūbu region, have long been blessed with a great abundance of fresh seafoods. The inland districts of these regions, however, have been restricted to freshwater fish and plants and herbs grown in the mountains. Both regions developed later than the ancient imperial capital of Kyoto, which has something of an edge when it comes to culinary elegance, but both regions have their partisans.

Kenuki-zushi was created in the Kanda district of Edo in 1702. Rice and fish are placed on and then wrapped in bamboo leaves.

Kenshin-zushi is made in Kofu, Yamanashi Prefecture. It is named after Uesugi Kenshin (1530–78), a famous general who in later life became a Buddhist priest. Instead of fish, it makes use of *sansai*, mountain plants that grow wild. The bamboo leaf is decorative and inedible.

111

Kinki

Tradition-minded Kyoto, a city with a 1200-year history, was the part of the Kinki region where such refined cuisines as Buddhist vegetarian cooking and the tea-ceremony *kaiseki* meal evolved.

Nearby Osaka is noted for its robust foods and has the reputation of being a city where the citizens go to any length to eat plenty and well. *Nare-zushi*, the forerunner of all later sushi, is still prepared in Nara, Mie and Wakayama prefectures.

The *funa-zushi* of the Kinki region takes from 6 months to 1 year to make. When it is ready to be eaten, it is sliced as shown in the photograph at the right.

Kodai suzume-zushi is a specialty of the Sushi-man shop in Osaka. The firm fillets of the *kodai* (small sea bream) used in this sushi, which has been made from a long time ago, are a beautiful pink.

Osaka *battera* sushi is a great favorite in the Kansai region. Mackerel is well salted, allowed to stand for 7 or 8 hours, then washed and marinated in a vinegar mixture before being pressed between layers of rice.

Hokuriku and Chūgoku

Kanazawa, the castle town of the very prosperous Maeda lords of Kaga, is the home of exquisite Kutani porcelain and opulent *Kaga-yūzen* dyed fabrics. The Kanazawa style of food is as eye-catching and sumptuous as these two famous local products. Developed under the influence of Kyoto cuisine, Kanazawa's dishes are a refined combination of delicacies from the Japan Sea and vegetables and herbs from field and mountain.

The Chūgoku region in western Honshu, famous for economic stability and its gentle climate, offers another luxurious cuisine featuring seafoods from the waters of the Seto Inland Sea.

Shikoku and Kyushu

Living on an island between the Seto Inland Sea and the Black Current of the Pacific Ocean, the people of Shikoku enjoy a wealth of food from the sea and an abundant harvest of agricultural products in a rich local cuisine.

Further to the west, the island of Kyushu was for centuries remote from the main centers of Japanese cultural evolution and developed its own life-styles and foods. The only part of Japan where foreigners were permitted during the period of isolation the nation experienced from the 17th to the 19th centuries, Kyushu has a cuisine blending native and foreign elements.

In Toyama Prefecture, *masu-zushi* is made by placing rice on a bamboo leaf. Fish is then placed on the rice and the leaf is folded up and over. The sushi is pressed in a frame (like the one at right center) or in round trays weighted with a rock.

To make the *ōmura-zushi* of Kyushu, a layer of fish is placed in the middle of the rice as well as on top. The whole is topped with omelet.

Sushi Shops Around the World

Australia

Kabuki No. 2
98 Bourke St.
Woolloomooloo
Sydney
358–2245

Keisan
Menzies Hotel
14 Carrington St.
Sydney
2–0232

Kyoto Restaurant
Cremorne Plaza
342 Military Rd.
Cremorne
Sydney
909–3865

Nagoya Sukiyaki House
188 Victoria St.
Kings Cross
Sydney
358–1711

Restaurant Suntory
529 Kent St.
Sydney
267–2900

Suehiro
157 Walker St.
North Sydney
922–5744

Sukiyaki Tokyo
1 Earl Place
Kings Cross
Sydney
358–5850

Canada

Aki
374 Powell St.
Vancouver, B. C.
682–4032

Aki No. 2
660 East Hastings St.
Vancouver, B. C.
254–5235

Jinya
567 West Broadway
Vancouver, B. C.
873–5040

Kameizushi
811 Thurlow St.
Vancouver, B. C.
684–4823

Koji
601 West Broadway
Vancouver, B. C.
876–3727

Koji
347 East Hastings St.
Vancouver, B. C.
689–7351

Matsuba
745 Thurlow St.
Vancouver, B. C.
681–5616

Yoshi
745 Thurlow St.
Vancouver, B. C.
683–5113

England

Azami
13–15 West St.
London
240–0634

Defune
61 Blandford St.
London W1
935–8311

Eikokukaku
9 Walbrook
London E. C. 4
236–9020

Hana-Guruma
49 Bow Lane
London E. C. 4
236–6452

Ikeda
30 Brook St.
London W1
629–2730

Mikado
110 George St.
London W1
935–8320

Sakura
9 Hanover St.
London W1
629–2961

Sushimasa
6–8 St. Christopher's
Place
London W1
935–1579

France

Ai
20 av. de l'Opera
Paris 1e
296 0137

Hanabusa
4 passage de la
Petite Boucherie
Paris 6e
326 5029

Ise
56 rue Ste. Anne
Paris 2e
296 6776

Kabuki
9 rue de la Gaité
Paris 14e
320 0478

Ogura
20 rue de la Michodière
Paris 2e
742 7779

Sakura
5 rue du Hanovre
Paris 2e
742 8258

Suntory
13 rue Lincoln
Paris 8e
225 4027

Takara
14 rue Molière
Paris 1e
296 0838

Yamato
Hotel Meridien
81 Bd Gouvion
St. Cyr, Paris 17ᵉ
758 1230

Holland

Toga
Weteringschans 128
Amsterdam
020–226829

Yamazato
Hotel Okura
Ferdinand Bolstraat 175
1072 LH Amsterdam
020–787111

Italy

Hamasei
Via della Mercede 35–36
Rome
6792134

Nihonbashi
Via Torino 34
Rome
4756970

Tokyo Restaurant
Via di Propaganda 22
Rome
6783942

Japan

AICHI PREF.

Tanaka-zushi Honten
4–12 Sakae 1 chōme
Naka-ku
Nagoya
201–2550

AKITA PREF.

Fuku-zushi
2–25 Ōmachi 3 chōme
Akita
23–7374

AOMORI PREF.

Takara-zushi
17–14 Furukawa
1 chōme
Aomori
22–5600

CHIBA PREF.

Takei Honten
5–7 Chūō 3 chōme
Chiba
222–1921

EHIME PREF.

Sushimaru
3–2 Niban-chō 2 chōme
Matsuyama
41–0449

FUKUI PREF.

Daruma-zushi
5–19 Bunkyō 4 chōme
Fukui
22–2574

FUKUOKA PREF.

Mikuniya
13 Gokusho-Machi 9 chōme
Hakata-ku
Fukuoka
271-2712

FUKUSHIMA PREF.

Chiyo-zushi
8 Honchō 1 chōme
Fukushima
22–1414

GIFU PREF.

Sushiyasu Honten
1 Hinode-chō
Gifu
62–0460

GUMMA PREF.

Sanmanryō
6–2 Chiyoda-chō
4 chōme
Maebashi
31–2543

HIROSHIMA PREF.

Kogane-zushi
2 Horikawa-chō
6 chōme
Hiroshima
247–3131

HOKKAIDO PREF.

Matsu-zushi
15 chōme Shijō
Asahikawa
23–5521

HYŌGO PREF.

Akashiya
8–21 Okamoto-chō
1 chōme
Higashi Nada-ku
Kobe
451–4551

Fuku-zushi
4–22 Shinkaichi
3 chōme
Hyōgo-ku
Kobe
575–2907

Harukoma
14–18 Motomachi-dōri
1 chōme
Chūō-ku
Kobe
331–8610

Sarashina
8–12 Ōtsuka-chō
1 chōme
Nagata-ku
Kobe
691–2175

Sushitake
3–9 Sumadera-chō
2 chōme
Suma-ku
Kobe
731–1005

Taikō
2 Shimo Yamate-dōri
6 chōme
Chūō-ku
Kobe
341–6834

Uoyoshi
1–17 Morigo-chō
2 chōme
Nada-ku
Kobe
851–2096

IBARAKI PREF.

Kaneki-zushi
18–10 Shimo Takatsu-
chō 1 chōme
Tsuchiura
22–8912

ISHIKAWA PREF.

Sushisei
6–25 Honchō 2 chōme
Kanazawa
21–6759

IWATE PREF.

Janome Honten
8 Sakae-chō 2 chōme
Miyako
2–1383

KAGAWA PREF.

Tsunohachi-zushi

9–35 Nishichō 2 chōme
Takamatsu
21–7082

KAGOSHIMA PREF.

Yōki-zushi

5 Meizan-chō 3 chōme
Kagoshima
22–5652

KANAGAWA PREF.

Fuku-zushi

7–17 Fuchinobe
 3 chōme
Sagamihara
52–2193

KUMAMOTO PREF.

Daruma-zushi

23 Shin Shigai 6 chōme
Kumamoto
52–8067

KYOTO PREF.

Azuma-zushi

Shimo Tateuri Agaru
Senbon-dōri
Kamigyō-ku, Kyoto
841–5756

Hisago

Takoyakushi Sagaru
Kawaramachi-dōri
Nakagyō-ku, Kyoto
221–1404

Isami

Nishiki-kōji Sagaru
Shin Kyōgoku-dōri
Nakagyō-ku, Kyoto
221–1331

Izū

Kiyomoto-chō, Yasaka
 Shinchi Gion
Higashiyama-ku, Kyoto
561–0751

Janome

Sanjō Sagaru
Shin Kyōgoku-dōri
Nakagyō-ku, Kyoto
221–1437

Jūbē

Shinbashi Agaru
Nawate-dōri
Higashiyama-ku, Kyoto
551–1333

Jūbē

1 Higashi Honchō
 8 chōme, Shimokamo
Sakyō-ku, Kyoto
791–0451

Otowa

Shijō Agaru
Shin Kyōgoku-dōri
Nakagyō-ku, Kyoto
221–2471

Sankichi

Kami Juzuya-machi
 Sagaru, Higashi Tōin-
 dōri
Shimogyō-ku, Kyoto
371–7684

Sushitora

Senbon Nishiiru
Imadegawa-dōri
Kamigyō-ku, Kyoto
462–0615

MIE PREF.

Yakko-zushi

10 Suwa Sakae-machi
 6 chōme
Yokkaichi
53–1528

MIYAGI PREF.

Fuku-zushi

3–31 Ichiban-chō
 4 chōme
Sendai
22–6326

MIYAZAKI PREF.

Kamehachi-zushi

Nishi Tachibana-dōri
Miyazaki
22–5455

NAGANO PREF.

Kamome-zushi

2337 Gondō-chō
Nagano
32–4613

NAGASAKI PREF.

Yoshimune

2709 Honkawauchi
Nagasaki
23–4272

NIIGATA PREF.

Miya-zushi

76 Asahi-machi 1 chōme
Niigata
28–8116

ŌITA PREF.

Yasuke-zushi

Honjō-chō
Hita
2–2216

OKAYAMA PREF.

Uotaki

15 Koshō-machi
Tsuyama
22–3154

OKINAWA PREF.

Kappō Matsufuku

457 Asato
Naha
63–1180

OSAKA PREF.

Fuku-zushi

1–11 Uchi Honmachi
 2 chōme
Suita
381–1819

Fuminosato Matsu-zushi

1–5 Fuminosato
 4 chōme
Abeno-ku
Osaka
629–0074

Futami-zushi

8–21 Ebie 2 chōme
Fukushima-ku
Osaka
451–4587

Matsushin

674–3 Shinkawa
 2 chōme
Naniwa-ku
Osaka
633–0459

Matsu-zushi

61 Kohama Higashino-
 chō 4 chōme
Sumiyoshi-ku
Osaka
671–5606

Sanpei-zushi

9–19 Jūsō Higashi
 2 chōme
Yodogawa-ku
Osaka
303–3262

Sushigen

26 Nanba Shinchi
 1 chōme
Minami-ku
Osaka
211–4450

Tokiwa-zushi

9–3 Shinmachi
 3 chōme
Nishi-ku
Osaka
531–6028

Tomiya
12–25 Honjō Nishi
  1 chōme
Ōyodo-ku
Osaka
371–1491

Toyoshin
13–16 Nakatsu 1 chōme
Ōyodo-ku
Osaka
374–0015

SAITAMA PREF.

Genroku
6–24 Honchō 3 chōme
Kawaguchi
22–3784

SHIGA PREF.

Fukusuke-zushi
7–27 Nagara 2 chōme
Ōtsu
24–3231

SHIZUOKA PREF.

Sushitetsu Honten
4–5 Ryōgae-chō
  2 chōme
Shizuoka
55–3551

TOCHIGI PREF.

Shinsei-kan
3–6 Baba-machi
  2 chōme
Utsunomiya
35–9100

TOKUSHIMA PREF.

Tarafuku
11 Shinnai-chō 1 chōme
Tokushima
22–3339

TOKYO

Bentenyama Miyako
1–16 Asakusa 2 chōme
Taitō-ku
Tokyo
3844–0034

Daigo
1–4 Den'enchōfu
  3 chōme
Ōta-ku
Tokyo
3721–9355

Edo-zushi
28–8 Jiyūgaoka 1 chōme
Meguro-ku
Tokyo
3717–5113

Fuku-zushi
7–8 Roppongi 5 chōme
Minato-ku
Tokyo
3402–4116

Ginza Benkay
2–17 Ginza 7 chōme
Chūō-ku
Tokyo
3573–7335

Gin-zushi
5–14 Kiba 5 chōme
Kōtō-ku
Tokyo
3641–4825

Hōrai
6–13 Nihonbashi
  3 chōme
Chūō-ku
Tokyo
3281–8851

Hōrai-zushi Honten
4–3 Asakusa 1 chōme
Taitō-ku
Tokyo
3841–7471

Iroha-zushi
11–3 Ueno 6 chōme
Taitō-ku
Tokyo
3831–3653

Janoichi
7 Nihonbashi Muro-chō
  6 chōme
Chūō-ku
Tokyo
3241–3566

Kaga-zushi
10–1 Shinjuku 6 chōme
Shinjuku-ku
Tokyo
3354–5431

Kiku-zushi
9–11 Takanawa 3 chōme
Minato-ku
Tokyo
3441–8891

Kin-zushi
10–16 Maruyama-chō
Shibuya-ku
Tokyo
3461–6600

Kitaichi-zushi
28–6 Kita Shinagawa
  1 chōme
Shinagawa-ku
Tokyo
3471–4860

Kiyota
3–15 Ginza 6 chōme
Chūō-ku
Tokyo
3572–4854

Kurataya
1–2 Otowa 2 chōme
Bunkyō-ku
Tokyo
3941–2741

Kyūbe
5–23 Ginza 8 chōme
Chūō-ku
Tokyo
3571–6523

Marukin-zushi
27–3 Higashi Gotanda
  5 chōme
Shinagawa-ku
Tokyo
3442–6469

Midori-zushi
2-4 Kyōdō 2 chōme
Setagaya-ku
Tokyo
3420–4078

Murai
1–3 Shiba 5 chōme
Minato-ku
Tokyo
3451–6772

Nakata
7–19 Ginza
Chūō-ku
Tokyo
3571–0063

Okei-zushi
8–11 Yaesu 1 chōme
Chūō-ku
Tokyo
3271–9928

Ōkuni-zushi Honten
7–30 Minami Azabu
  2 chōme
Minato-ku
Tokyo
3453–2726

Ōzushi

7–5 Shibuya 1 chōme
Shibuya-ku
Tokyo
3400–2221

Sakae-zushi

31–15 Kitazawa
   2 chōme
Setagaya-ku
Tokyo
3468–0009

Sakae-zushi

9–20 Hatagaya 2 chōme
Shibuya-ku
Tokyo
3377–4484

Sakae-zushi Shōkichi

2–7 Shimura 1 chōme
Itabashi-ku
Tokyo
3965–9229

Suehiro-zushi

4–10 Higashi Komagata
   3 chōme
Sumida-ku
Tokyo
3622–4604

Sushiei

13–2 Ginza 7 chōme
Chūō-ku
Tokyo
3541–5055

Sushiharu

20–6 Haneda 4 chōme
Ōta-ku
Tokyo
3741–0808

Sushihatsu Sohonten

12–10 Asakusa 1 chōme
Taitō-ku
Tokyo
3842–0777

Sushikō

3–8 Ginza 6 chōme
Chūō-ku
Tokyo
3571–1968

Sushimasa

1–26 Shin Koiwa
   2 chōme
Katsushika-ku
Tokyo
3651–0737

Sushisen

6–9 Ginza 8 chōme
Chūō-ku
Tokyo
3571–3288

Sushitsune

10–8 Meguro 2 chōme
Meguro-ku
Tokyo
3492–2041

Sushizen

3–12 Nishi Ikebukuro
   4 chōme
Toshima-ku
Tokyo
3981–2708

Takara-zushi

2 Ōyama-chō 9 chōme
Itabashi-ku
Tokyo
3956–1787

Shin-Takase

11–7 Negishi 3 chōme
Taitō-ku
Tokyo
3873–4757

Take-zushi

10–2 Ginza 5 chōme
Chūō-ku
Tokyo
3543–2241

Tamagawa-zushi

19–4 Jingūmae 1 chōme
Shibuya-ku
Tokyo
3401–0888

Tama-zushi

39–3 Nakano 3 chōme
Nakano-ku
Tokyo
3383–3355

Tama-zushi

9–4 Tsukiji 1 chōme
Chūō-ku
Tokyo
3541–1917

Tomoeya

32–6 Sangenjaya
   1 chōme
Setagaya-ku
Tokyo
3421–3548

Yoroi-zushi

18–11 Hyakunin-chō
   1 chōme
Shinjuku-ku
Tokyo
3363–8006

Yoshino

6–5 Kyōbashi 3 chōme
Chūō-ku
Tokyo
3561–3676

Yoshino-zushi

8–11 Nihonbashi
   3 chōme
Chūō-ku
Tokyo
3274–3001

TOTTORI PREF.

Ko-zushi

509 Sakae-chō
Tottori
22–5535

TOYAMA PREF.

Miki-zushi Honten

7 Sakura-chō 1 chōme
Toyama
32–7201

YAMAGATA PREF.

Tatsu-zushi

1–30 Nanoka-machi
4 chōme
Yamagata
22–4597

YAMAGUCHI PREF.

Chidori-zushi

23 Jōtō-chō 2 ban
Ube
32–5303

YAMANASHI PREF.

Jisaku-zushi

8–19 Chūō-ku 4 chōme
Kōfu
35–1238

Mexico

Daikoku

Michoacán 25
México, D. F.
584–85–57

Fuji

Río Pánuco 128
México 5, D. F.
514–68–14

Suntory

Torres Adalid 14
México 12, D. F.
536–77–54

The Philippines

Aoi

Century Ceraton Park
Hotel
Manila
50–60–41

Benkay

Manila Garden Hotel
Manila
85–79–11

Furusato

Roxas Blvd.
Manila
59–74–21

Kappo Kaneko

Makati Ave.
Makati
85–44–14

Koto Restaurant

1151 M. H. Delpilar
Manila
58–90–88

Misono

Hyatt of Manila Hotel
Manila
80–26–11

New Tokyo

691 Makati Ave.
Makati
87–11–53

Serina

100 Jupiter St.
Belair, Makati
86–29–76

Sugi Restaurant

1151 M. H. Delpilar
Manila

Singapore

Hoshigaoka

Apollo Hotel
405/407 Hovelock Rd.
Singapore
432081

Kaiho

Milamar Hotel
Singapore
910222

Kanakana

York Hotel
21 Mount Elizabeth
Singapore
7370511

Kanako

Good Wood Park Hotel
22 Scotts Rd.
Singapore
7377411

Kanpachi

Equatrial Hotel
Singapore
2560431

Kiku

Orchid Inn
Singapore
2531122

Tsurunoya

Mandarin Hotel
Singapore
7374411

Unkai

Century Park Sheraton
Hotel
Nass'm Hill
Singapore
7379677

Yamagen

36 Orchard Street
Singapore

Thailand

Akamon

233 Soi Asoke
Sukhumvit Rd.
Bangkok
391–8144

Daikoku

960 Rama 4 Rd.
Saladaeng
Bangkok
233–1495

Goro

399/1 Soi Siri
Silom Rd.
Bangkok
234–1001

Hanaya

683 Siphya Rd.
Bangkok
233–3080

Kikusui

133 Punt Rd.
Silom Rd.
Bangkok
234–4031

Kyoto
9 Sukhumvit Soi 11
Sukhumvit Rd.
Bangkok
252-8458

Matsuko
Amarin Hotel
526 Ploenchit Rd.
Bangkok
252-9810

Naniwa
58/11 Soi Thaniya
Silom Rd.
Bangkok
235-2736

Seto
Thai Daimaru
95 Rajdamri Rd.
Bangkok
251-9151

Shin Hakata
6/L Rama 4 Rd.
Bangkok
233-6535

Tokugawa
Ambassador Hotel
Sukhumvit Soi 11
Sukhumvit Rd.
Bangkok
251-5151

Tsukiji
62/15-16 Thaniya Rd.
Bangkok
234-2414

United States

CALIFORNIA

Los Angeles

Amagi
6114 Sunset Blvd.
Hollywood, Cal.
464-7497

Asuka
1266 Westwood Blvd.
West Los Angeles, Cal.
474-7412

Bukyu
242 East 2nd St.
Los Angeles, Cal.
687-3678

Cher-Ton-Ton
316 Pier Ave
Hermosa Beach, Cal.
372-8917

Demekin
216 West Garvey Ave.
Monterey Park, Cal.
571-9029

Domo
11680 Ventura Blvd.
Studio City, Cal.
761-6151

Eigiku Cafe
314 East 1st St.
Los Angeles, Cal.
629-3029

Eiko Sukiyaki
806 West Carson St.
Torrance, Cal.
320-9012

Hama Sushi
347 East 2nd St.
Los Angeles, Cal.
680-3454

Hamayoshi
3350 West 1st St.
Los Angeles, Cal.
384-2914

Hana Sushi
11831 Wilshire Blvd.
Los Angeles, Cal.
477-9796

Hiro Sushi
1621 Wilshire Blvd.
Santa Monica, Cal.
395-3570

Horikawa
111 South San Pedro St.
Los Angeles, Cal.
680-9355

Horikawa Restaurant
250 East 1st St.
Los Angeles, Cal.
557-2531

Ichiban
108 South San Pedro St.
Los Angeles, Cal.
622-4453

Imperial Gardens
8225 Sunset Blvd.
West Hollywood, Cal.
656-1750

Inagiku Restaurant
Bonaventure Hotel
404 South Figueroa St.
Los Angeles, Cal.
614-0820

Kanpachi
14813 South Western
  Ave.
Gardena, Cal.
515-1391

Kawafuku
1636 West Redondo
  Beach Blvd.
Gardena, Cal.
770-3637

Kiku of Tokyo
930 Wilshire Blvd.
Los Angeles, Cal.
628-3176

Kikusai Restaurant
1809 South Catalina
  Ave.
Redondo Beach, Cal.
375-1244

Kinjo
980 North La Cienega
  Blvd.
Los Angeles, Cal.
652-2443

Koetsu
12531 Alondra Blvd.
Norwalk, Cal.
921-0206

Koto Restaurant
4300 Van Karman Ave.
Newport Beach, Cal.
752-7151

Kyotaro
8649 Firestone Blvd.
Downey, Cal.
869-1171

Kyoto Sukiyaki
15122 South Western
  Ave.
Gardena, Cal.
515-9575

Masukawa Sushi
1328 Rosecrans
Gardena, Cal.
323-1922

Matoi
8400 Santa Monica Blvd.
Los Angeles, Cal.
654-0945

Matsuno Sushi
313 East 1st St.
Los Angeles, Cal.
628-8816

Matsu Sushi
6405 Wilshire Blvd.
Los Angeles, Cal.
852–1915

Mitsuwa Restaurant
10645 West Pico Blvd.
West Los Angeles, Cal.
475–0117

Naniwa
137 Japanese Village
  Plaza
Los Angeles, Cal.
623–3661

Narikoma
11697 Del Amo Blvd.
Lakewood, Cal.
865–4229

Nippontei Restaurant
717 North Broadway St.
Los Angeles, Cal.
628–1481

Noda Restaurant
249 East Foothill Blvd.
Arcadia, Cal.
359–7116

Noma Restaurant
2031 Wilshire Blvd.
Santa Monica, Cal.
397–8548

Oban
14419 Pioneer Blvd.
Norwalk, Cal.
864–7217

Okada
517 West 7th St.
Los Angeles, Cal.
689–1241

Oomasa
100 Japanese Village
  Plaza Mall
Los Angeles, Cal.
623–9040

Osho Sushi
10914 West Pico Blvd.
West Los Angeles, Cal.
475–3226

Restaurant Eisaku
5511 Orange Thorpe
  Ave.
La Palma, Cal.
522–3792

Restaurant Enshino
17049 Ventura Blvd.
Encino, Cal.
783–4621

Restaurant Genji
310 Washington Blvd.
Marina del Rey, Cal.
822–5152

Restaurant Plaza
356 East 1st St.
Los Angeles, Cal.
628–0697

Restaurant Tabiji
2806 West Ball Rd.
Anaheim, Cal.
995–6432

Restaurant Tokyo
510 West 6th St.
Los Angeles, Cal.
624–5491

Restaurant Tokyo
9561 Wilshire Blvd.
Beverly Hills, Cal.
274–7568

Restaurant Tokyo
621 South Olive
Los Angeles, Cal.
687–9606

Restaurant Tsukasa
23532 El Toro Rd.
El Toro Orange Tree
  Plaza
Los Angeles, Cal.
770–6147

Restaurant Yae
11616 Iberia Place
Rancho Bernardo, Cal.
485–0390

Restaurant Zakuro
11703 The Plaza
Norwalk, Cal.
863–0170

Sheraton Hotel
La Reina
6101 West Century
  Blvd.
Los Angeles, Cal.
642–1111

Shibucho
3114 Beverly Blvd.
Los Angeles, Cal.
387–8498

Shihoya
15489 Ventura Blvd.
Sherman Oaks, Cal.
986–4461

Shima
816 South Atlantic Blvd.
Monterey Park, Cal.
576–9846

Shinano
1106 South Atlantic
  Blvd.
Monterey Park, Cal.
283–0026

Shogun
470 Halstead St.
Pasadena, Cal.
351–8945

Sushi Ichiban
2195 South Garfield
  Ave.
Monterey Park, Cal.
723–1856

Sushi-Katsu
2350 West Lomita Blvd.
Lomita, Cal.
539–2764

Sushi-Ko
2932½ Beverly Glen
Los Angeles, Cal.
475–8689

Teru Sushi
11940 Ventura Blvd.
Studio City, Cal.
763–6201

A Thousand Cranes
120 South Los Angeles
  St.
Los Angeles, Cal.
629–1200

Tokyo Kaikan Restaurant
225 South San Pedro St.
Los Angeles, Cal.
489–1333

Tokyo Sukiyaki
1333 West Gonzales Rd.
Oxnard, Cal.
485–7337

Tomi-san
2506½ East 1st St.
Los Angeles, Cal.
268–2421

Yagura Ichiban
101 Japanese Village
  Plaza
Los Angeles, Cal.
623–4141

Yamato
2025 Avenue of the
  Stars
Los Angeles, Cal.
277–1840

Yasubays Restaurant
1219 South Saviers Rd.
Oxnard, Cal.
483–9611

Yoko Sushi House
3862 Crenshaw Blvd.
Los Angeles, Cal.
296–9397

San Francisco and Northern California

Cho Cho Restaurant
1020 Kearny St.
San Francisco, Cal.
397-3066

Fuki Sushi
4119 El Camino Real
Palo Alto, Cal.
494-9383

Fuki Ya
22 Peace Plaza
San Francisco, Cal.
929-0174

Fuku Sushi
1580 Webster St.
San Francisco, Cal.
346-3030

Goemon
1524 Irving St.
San Francisco, Cal.
664-2288

Hama Sushi
30050 Stevens Creek
    Rd.
Cupertino, Cal.
252-9446

Ichibankan
3347 Fillmore St.
San Francisco, Cal.
567-1888

Inaka Sushi
West and Shaw St.
Fresno, Cal.
439-7816

Ino Sushi
1620 Webster St.
San Francisco, Cal.
922-3121

Kame Sushi
1581 Webster St.
San Francisco, Cal.

Kansai Restaurant
325 Sacramento St.
San Francisco, Cal.
392-2648

Kantoh Teriyaki
160 Ellis St.
San Francisco, Cal.
391-8494

Kichihei
2084 Chestnut St.
San Francisco, Cal.
929-1670

Kikkyo Restaurant
2339 Fremont St.
Monterey, Cal.
372-5440

Kiku of Tokyo
San Francisco Hilton
    Hotel
333 O'Farrel St.
San Francisco, Cal.
441-5458

Kinokawa Restaurant
347 Grant Ave.
San Francisco, Cal.
956-6085

Koharu
47 East 4th St.
San Mateo, Cal.
348-0654

Kokeshi
1306 Saratoga Ave.
San Jose, Cal.
249-6020

Komatsu
93 South Central Ave.
Campbell, Cal.
379-3000

Matsu
299 Baldwin St.
San Mateo, Cal.
347-5567

Matsuya
3856 24th St.
San Francisco, Cal.
282-7989

Misono Restaurant
1737 Post St.
San Francisco, Cal.
922-2728

Nikko Sukiyaki
1450 Van Ness Ave.
San Francisco, Cal.
474-7722

Osome
1946 Fillmore St.
San Francisco, Cal.
346-2311

Otafuku Tei
1737 Buchanan St.
San Francisco, Cal.
931-1578

Sanpei Restaurant
1581 Webster St.
San Francisco, Cal.
922-2290

Sanpoo
1702 Post St.
San Francisco, Cal.
346-3486

Serina
5116 Geary St.
San Francisco, Cal.
752-5652

Sugata
1105 Solano St.
Albany, Cal.
526-3516

Sushi Gen
107 Garedonia St.
Sausalito, Cal.
332-2284

Sushi Man
731 Bush St.
San Francisco, Cal.
981-1313

Takuwan
1750 Buchanan St.
San Francisco, Cal.
567-6685

Tokyo Sukiyaki
225 Jefferson St.
San Francisco, Cal.
775-9030

Toraya
1734 Post St.
San Francisco, Cal.
931-5200

Waraku Restaurant
22 Peace Plaza
San Francisco, Cal.
346-2265

Yamato Sukiyaki
717 California St.
San Francisco, Cal.
397-3456

Yoshi
6030 Claremont St.
Oakland, Cal.
652-9200

HAWAII

Furusato No. 1
Waikiki Grand
134 Kapahulu Ave.
Honolulu, Hawaii
923-8878

Furusato No. 2
Hyatt Regency Hotel
2424 Kalakaua Ave.
Honolulu, Hawaii
922-4991

Furusato No. 3
Foster Tower
2500 Kalakaua Ave.
Honolulu, Hawaii
922-5502

Kyoya
2057 Kalakaua Ave.
Honolulu, Hawaii
947-3911

Maiko No. 1
Ilikai Hotel
1777 Ala Moana Blvd.
Honolulu, Hawaii
946-5151

Maiko No. 2
131 Kaiulani Ave.
Honolulu, Hawaii
923-7368

New Tokyo
286 Beach Walk
Honolulu, Hawaii
923-8411

Santori
Royal Hawaiian Shop-
    ping Center
Honolulu, Hawaii
922-5511

ILLINOIS

Edoya
1285 South Elmhurst
Rd.
Des Plaines, Ill.
593-2470

Happi Sushi
3346 North Clark St.
Chicago, Ill.
528-1225

Hashikin
2338 North Clark St.
Chicago, Ill.
935-6474

Hatsuhana
160 East Ontario St.
Chicago, Ill.
280-8287

Kabuki of Chicago
101 East Ontario
Chicago, Ill.
266-7733

Kamehachi
1617 North Wells
Chicago, Ill.
664-3663

Sakura
105 South Main St.
Mt. Prospect, Ill.
259-0444

Torishin
1584 South Busse Rd.
Mt. Prospect, Ill.
437-4590

Yanase
818 North State St.
Chicago, Ill.
337-9598

NEW YORK

Akasaka
715 2nd Ave.
New York, N. Y.
867-6410

Akita
12 East 44th St.
New York, N. Y.
697-0342

Asahi
1475 Bergen Blvd.
Fort Lee, N. J.
944-5113

Edo
7 West 46th St.
New York, N. Y.
719-4213

Edo Garden
104 Washington St.
New York, N. Y.
344-2583

Enka
147 West 45th St.
New York, N. Y.
247-5543

Ginrei
148 East 50th St.
New York, N. Y.
759-7454

Hatsuhana
17 East 48th St.
New York, N. Y.
355-3345

Iroha
731 7th Ave.
New York, N. Y.
398-9049

Izakaya
43 West 54th St.
New York, N. Y.
765-4683

Jinyazushi
123 West 49th St.
New York, N. Y.
245-4094

Kamehachi
14 East 47th St.
New York, N. Y.
765-4737

Kamon
302 Columbus Ave.
New York, N. Y.
874-8278

Kiraku
127 East 56th St.
New York, N. Y.
751-1088

Lenge
202 Columbus Ave.
New York, N. Y.
874-8278

Kurumazushi
423 Madison Ave.
New York, N. Y.
751-5258

Mie Restaurant
196 2nd Ave.
New York, N. Y.
674-7060

Mint of Orient
1013 2nd Ave.
New York, N. Y.
751-4322

Miyokawa
23 West 56th St.
New York, N. Y.
586-6899

Mitsukoshi
465 Park Ave.
New York, N. Y.
935-6444

Mugi
132 West 58th St.
New York, N. Y.
757-5842

Nadazushi
135 East 50th St.
New York, N. Y.
838-2537

Nakagawa
7 West 44th St.
New York, N. Y.
869-8077

Nippon
145 East 52nd St.
New York, N. Y.
758-0226

Rikyu
210 Columbus Ave.
New York, N. Y.
799-7847

Sagano
3 East 44th St.
New York, N. Y.
986-1355

Saito
305 East 46th St.
New York, N. Y.
759-8897

Shinbashi
280 Park Ave.
New York, N. Y.
661-3915

Shiro of Japan
401 Old Country Rd.
Carle Place, N. Y.
997-4770

Sushiginza
4 East 46th St.
New York, N. Y.
687-4717

Sushikazu
41-32, Main St.
Flushing, N. Y.
939-4004

Sushiko
251 West 55th St.
New York, N. Y.
974-9721

Takezushi
11 East 48th St.
New York, N. Y.
755-6534

Takezushi West
101 West 45th St.
New York, N. Y.
391-1045

Yamaguchi
35 West 45th St.
New York, N. Y.
840-8185

Yamashiro
307 5th Ave.
New York, N. Y.
725-9241

Yodo
13 East 47th St.
New York, N. Y.
751-8775

Yokohama
47-01, Queens Blvd.
Sunnyside, N. Y.
784-9814

Yokohama West
58 West 56th St.
New York, N. Y.
582-6153

TEXAS

Benkay
5868 San Felipe
Houston, Tex.
785-0332

Fuji
11124 Westheimer
Houston, Tex.
789-4701

Tokyo Garden
4701 Westheimer
Houston, Tex.
622-7886

West Germany

Benkay
Immermanstr. 41
Dusseldorf
8661

Kikaku
Klosterstr. 38
Dusseldorf
357853

Nihonkan
Immermanstr. 35
Dusseldorf
353135

Yari
Oststr. 63
Dusseldorf
350213

Index

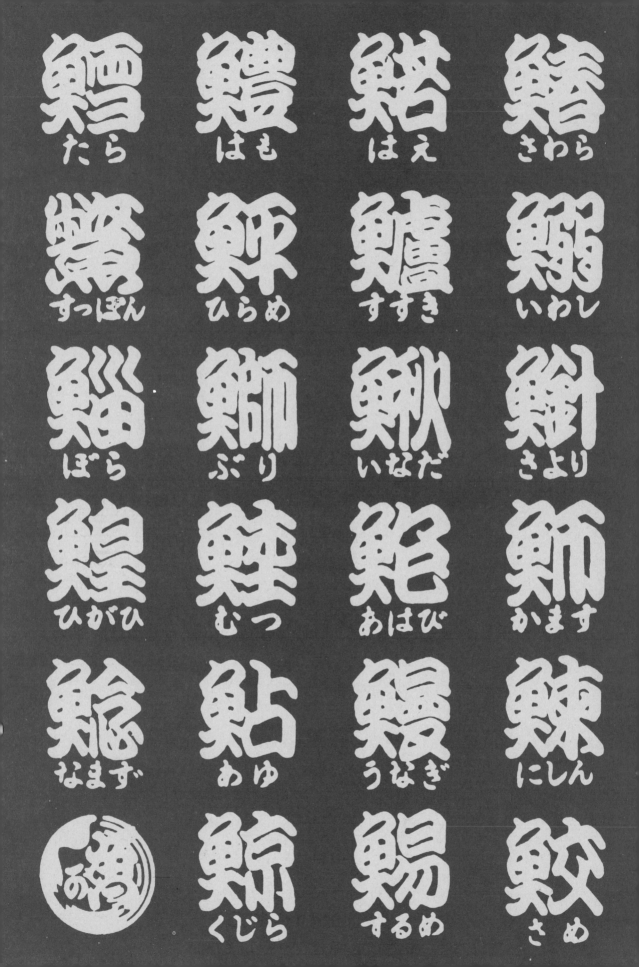

たら　はも　はえ　さわら

すっぽん　ひらめ　すずき　いわし

ぼら　ぶり　いなだ　さより

ひがひ　むつ　あはび　かます

なまず　あゆ　うなぎ　にしん

くじら　するめ　さめ